Gliding Competitively

John Delafield

Adam & Charles Black · London

First published 1982 by A & C Black (Publishers) Ltd
35 Bedford Row, London WC1R 4JH

© 1982 John Delafield

ISBN 0-7136-2224-5

Delafield, J
  Gliding competitively.
  1. Gliding and soaring
  I Title
  629.132′523   TL765

ISBN 0-7136-2224-5

Filmset in Apollo by
MS Filmsetting Ltd, Frome, Somerset

Printed and bound by
R J Acford, Chichester, Sussex

Contents

Contents

List of Illustrations

All photographs by John Delafield unless otherwise credited. All figures by Alan E. Bolton.

Photographs

Figures

List of illustrations

Foreword

The last ten to fifteen years have seen a significant growth in the number of books dedicated to the sport of competitive soaring and the enthusiastic newcomer need no longer complain of the lack of suitable material to assist him in fully realising his potential. Competition gliding is a complex and demanding sport, both technically and psychologically, and John Delafield is highly qualified to give detailed advice on how to prepare for, and fly in, the first all-important competition. John has represented Great Britain in several World Championships and he is one of the finest tacticians in the sport. He is also a highly motivated competitor and in reading this book one is struck by the attention to detail and the sheer professionalism of his approach.

No matter how well prepared the newcomer may be generally, it is very difficult to prepare for the psychological hurdles associated with flying in the first competition. There is often a tendency to under-estimate the importance of this aspect, and it is therefore all the more pleasing to find that John has included a detailed analysis of competition associated emotions.

Competitive soaring is one of the most challenging of individual sports, both mentally and physically – it must also be one of the most addictive! The newcomer will have his own reasons for wanting to give it a try but, whatever his motives, the attainment of his personal goal will be made a lot easier by the excellent material contained in this book.

George Lee

To my family

Preface

In this book, the term competitive gliding refers to racing gliding – the completion of closed circuit flights around specified turning points in the shortest possible time, where other pilots are also flying the same course. I am not concerned with height gains or duration flights, or with the business of cross-country record flying, although this has many connections with competition gliding.

I am writing for the pilot with basic experience who wants to succeed with task flying and competitions, and I have assumed that my readers will know most of the basics of soaring flight. The book is a training guide, with plenty of tips and advice based on my own experience. Broadly, each chapter represents a stage in a pilot's development, from local soaring through to competition flying, with the idea that he will be improving and developing his skills all the time. Some aspects are touched on early in the book and are developed more fully later, and to this extent there is a degree of overlap between chapters.

Competition gliding provides the impetus and opportunity for a pilot to stretch himself to his limits and realise his full potential. My aim in writing this book has been to stimulate a search for finesse and for achievement amongst my readers, but, above all, I hope that it will help *you* to avoid some of the many pitfalls I have encountered in my soaring experience.

John Delafield

Metrication

Wherever miles are quoted in the text, the reference is to nautical miles: therefore any metric equivalent must be calculated at 1 nautical mile = 1.85 kilometres *or* 1 kilometre = 0.54 nautical mile.

Metric measurements are now generally used in the gliding world, and all record and badge qualifying flights use metric terms. In the text, both imperial and metric distances are given. The conversion, however, is not intended to be precise: metric distances are suitably rounded in number, as exact equivalents would not be helpful, eg. 10 (nautical) miles is expressed as 20 kilometres rather than 18.5 kilometres.

1
Developing your flying
– local soaring

Consistently safe cross-country and competition gliding is built on the skills learnt through local flying at the home airfield and there is no justification for flying out of gliding range of your home site until you have fully mastered the fundamentals of gliding.

In particular, you must first learn to soar your glider under a wide variety of weather conditions. Second, you must be able to make consistently safe approaches and landings in different wind conditions and from difficult positions in the circuit pattern. And third, you must have received formal training in the techniques for making safe landings away from the home site, be it in English fields, Australian paddocks or Texan scrubland. To omit any one of these steps is to court disaster; a broken glider is probably the lowest price you can expect to pay.

In this chapter we will examine just a few ideas which you can usefully bear in mind whilst local soaring. You will gain much by putting them into effect whenever the opportunity arises; this will give your local soaring a worthwhile objective and will go a long way towards giving you the necessary background for successful competition flying. Some of the suggestions put forward here will be developed later in the book.

WEATHER CONDITIONS AND THERMAL
RECOGNITION

Clearly, the first requirement for successful soaring is to have suitable weather and it will be worthwhile spending time now in considering the main features of the most common cross-country soaring weather. With an appreciation of some of these points the soaring itself will prove to be that much easier.

Cumulus weather

To my mind, the most sought-after thermal soaring conditions come with a sky blossoming with cumulus clouds, evenly spaced every mile or so. Surely the weather glider pilots dream about? But, as with all things, soaring in such weather is not necessarily straight-forward and no two days will necessarily give the same conditions, however similar they may appear. It is essential, therefore, to appreciate the various extremes of soaring under conditions of cumulus cloud because between these extremes will be a myriad of different themal characteristics.

In simple terms, cumulus cloud can be associated with 'short-life' or 'long-life' thermals. In essence, short-lived cumulus clouds are characterised by their small size and by their generally frag-mented appearance. Short-life thermals associated with such clouds normally last for only a few minutes and are often linked with a particular thermal-producing source on the ground. Whilst their short duration can prove very troublesome – the thermal has gone by the time you get under the cloud – they have the advantage that the same ground source normally produces a steady series of thermals. In practice this means that if there appears to be no lift under your chosen cloud then the next thermal from the same source can often be located by flying into wind a little way.

Cumulus clouds associated with longer-lived thermals normally have a fairly substantial appearance; they can have a useful life, as regards lift-producing qualities, of about twenty minutes, sometimes

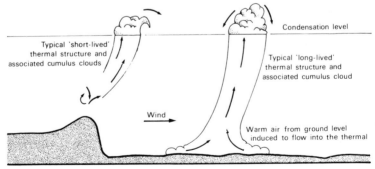

Figure 1. Diagram to illustrate the essential differences between 'short-lived' and 'long-lived' thermals and cumulus clouds

longer. Such clouds may well be formed initially by a thermal from an obvious source on the ground, but, once started, they sustain themselves by inducing further relatively buoyant air to break contact with the ground and flow into the thermal feeding the cloud in question. In general you can consider the thermals below such clouds to be columns, whereas the short-lived type should be thought of as bubbles. Figure 1 illustrates the essential differences.

Regardless of the type of cumulus, its lift-producing qualities can best be detected by very careful and painstaking observation of both its growth pattern and its general form. To be more specific as to what I mean by growth pattern, the give-away sign I always look for is movement or growth of the cloud itself. You can often see this best by closely watching the clouds and observing, on those producing lift, wisps of condensation displaying a rolling motion or at least showing clear signs of movement. This is not an infallible method but it normally works, especially for the smaller clouds. Large clouds tend to be easier to recognise for their lifting properties – the crisp-looking ones with solid-looking or firm dark bases are normally good but this generalisation does not always work and you therefore need to establish by trial and error a correlation between 'looks' as you perceive each cloud, and 'lift'. However, you can gain some comfort from the fact that even with large clouds, it is frequently possible to detect movement, particularly in their upper regions, and that this is often an indicator, though not an infallible one, of lift below their bases.

When you are flying it will often pay to operate somewhat below cloud base so that you can get a good perspective on possible lift-producing clouds, particularly their bases, because this will help you to better appreciate which ones are most likely to be active. Beware, however – clouds can still be active and lifting but you will sometimes find that the lift has decayed at the lower heights, so that if you plan to intercept the thermal related to such a cloud too low down you may be out of luck. In this case, by searching around below the cloud you may find a remnant to get you back up a few hundred feet and you may even intercept a fresh thermal travelling up the same path as the decayed one, but you must not rely on this.

When practising soaring under cumulus conditions I think the most important thing to aim for is to fly so as to gain an appreciation of the normal location of lift in relation to each particular type of cloud. In the case of very small clouds, particularly those which appear to have a rolling motion, the lift is often associated with the part of the cloud showing movement. But this will not always be the case and, therefore, you must go out to learn from experience the significance of the detailed shape and movement of the cloud in relation to the associated lift. With larger clouds of longer duration the problem is really twofold. First you must learn to appreciate the tell-tale signs of a cloud's growth and decay and second, you must learn where the likely areas of lift are in relation to the cloud. Small clouds, with their relatively small horizontal dimensions don't present too great a problem, but the area to be searched under a larger cloud for the core of any thermal makes it imperative that you learn to find the lift as early as possible if you are not to waste height and time. Remember that in a competitive situation someone else who can locate such lift more quickly than you will have a substantial advantage.

The lift associated with cumulus on any one day often follows a pattern, the lift being located in a similar position with each successive cloud. As a broad generalisation you can consider that the thermal is normally found a little into wind of the cloud: this is invariably a reasonable assumption to use at the beginning of any one flight although you may need to modify it in the light of experience on the day in question. In England, it seems to me, the lift is generally on the sunny side of most clouds, but I suspect that this is more likely due to the sun being on the same bearing as the prevailing wind during the normal soaring period (that is, south west) than to any other cause.

There are many variations in the positioning and characteristics of thermals associated with cumulus clouds and there is, therefore, almost no end to the worthwhile experience you can gain whilst soaring locally.

Cloud streets

Clouds often form linked lines which we call cloud streets. There are many types of cloud street; the 'classic', the convergence, and the wave influenced are amongst those most commonly met.

By considering just the 'classic' type we will cover the principles of using the other types as well, as they are very similar. Generally speaking, 'classic' cloud streets occur with moderate to fresh winds and with an optimum depth of convection for the air mass in

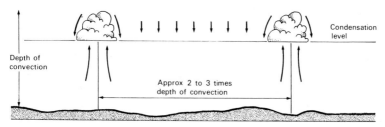

Figure 2. Cross section to show typical flow pattern around cloud streets (highly simplified)

question. Under these conditions they do not generally appear to originate from a particular source on the ground, but rather the cloud streets which result seem to be sustained by a larger scale flow within the convective layer and by the basic instability of the air mass itself. They may well be initiated in the first place by a series of ground sources but, as soon as any vertical development of the cloud takes place, the whole process becomes more or less self-sustaining. Figure 2 illustrates simply the type of large scale flow which is often associated with cloud streets.

Under 'streeting' conditions the relationship of the lift to the clouds can sometimes be confusing, especially when you are flying nearer to the ground than to the base of the cloud. Quite frequently under such conditions, the thermals will be choppy low down and distorted by the wind. Also, the lift may not be immediately below the bulk of the cloud street, but displaced to one side and forming apparently conventional thermal cells. Higher up, however, the lift normally becomes aligned with the cloud and is, therefore, easy to locate.

When practising local soaring, you will find it worthwhile to deliberately intercept the thermals associated with streets at different heights so that you can become familiar with the varied characteristics of such thermals.

Likewise, the distribution of lift along the axis of the street can take some getting used to and I suggest your practice takes the form of climbing in a thermal under the cloud until the lift begins to spread out under the street. Then, rather than continuing a circling climb, fly into the wind underneath the street to give yourself an opportunity to examine its structure. You will find that it will not give lift all the way, but the incidence of lift will be greater than the incidence of sink. As you proceed you should practise flying the correct speed as given by the 'speed to fly' facility on the vario-meter, having set the datum to a realistic thermal strength, and when you find a strong core you should then, and only then, take the climb up to within about 200 feet (60 metres) of the cloud base. The cruise along the street can be continued thereafter at the new, greater height.

I find that it sometimes pays to cruise under a street at less than the optimum speed to fly, as by so doing you can leave the street at maximum altitude, such as cloud base. This will be worth doing when conditions ahead look less straightforward than you would like and you believe that lift will be weak and perhaps difficult to find.

Once you have left your street you should bear in mind the likely air flow pattern (Figure 2) in transitting to your next lift source. Naturally, you should not forget the constraints of your local soaring practice flight as well, and some of what I have just described can be practised more readily on cross-country than on local flights. You must, however, make every effort to practise these techniques on local flights first.

Blue thermals

Flying in blue thermals is rather like walking through a forest with your eyes shut; you are bound to hit a tree sooner or later. If there is a problem of flying in the blue, though, it is that the convective layer is often shallow, certainly in England, although much less so in hotter climates, and therefore the effective *working* layer between the top of climb and the height at which you need to find the next thermal is relatively shallow. This implies that you may have to accept mediocre thermals purely to avoid dropping below the safe lower level for thermal contact. On the other hand, the location of blue thermals can often be more straightforward than cloud indicated ones. For a start, blue thermals tend to be more evenly distributed and they also tend to come off the type of source you would expect – such as villages, towns and other relatively hot spots. It follows, therefore, that your location of thermals in the blue must be influenced by the terrain below.

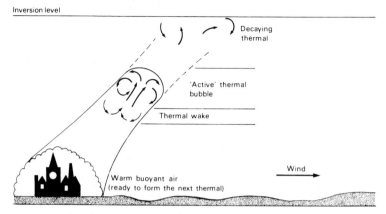

Figure 3.   Blue thermals – typical pattern

Blue thermals often take the form of bubbles, or series of bubbles, and this has a marked effect on the way in which you search them out. It will often pay not to rely on there being lift below another glider which you observe to be climbing well in a blue thermal; instead you will need to get used to the idea of flying into wind so as to intercept the *next* thermal from the same source. It will also pay dividends to actively think about likely thermal sources and to fly just downwind of them in order to locate any thermals which they may produce. Figure 3 shows a typical situation under blue conditions.

In moderate to fresh winds blue thermals tend to form themselves into streets. It is important to find out whether this is so as it has a significant bearing on how you locate each one and on how you progress in a desired direction.

On leaving the first thermal of your flight you should fly into the wind and, all being well, you should then find a continuous series of weaker thermals. Eventually you will encounter a strong one, probably at the end of the street, which you can use to regain height. You can then turn to fly in the desired direction, say, cross wind, and on encountering the next area of thermal-like turbulence you should turn into wind until you find a thermal. In this context the usual trick of turning towards the uplifted wing can be used to help you establish contact with the main axis of the thermal street. An air mass readout on the variometer is extremely useful under

7

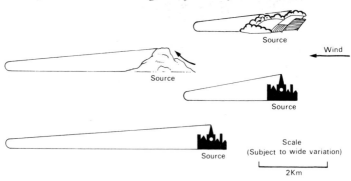

Figure 4.   Diagrammatic representation of 'blue' thermal streets

these conditions as it enables you to pinpoint readily the position of each street. Figure 4 is a simplified representation of blue thermal streets, which, from my own experience is broadly correct.

When flying in blue thermal streets, the main point to watch out for is the length of the streets and their lateral spacing. Neither can be relied upon – some streets are very short, especially those which appear to emanate from one particular source, whilst others seem to go on for miles.

Another feature which is common under blue thermal conditions is the tendency for the thermal to spread out near the top of its ascent as it hits the stabilising effect of the inversion. Whilst it will not normally pay to climb those last 500 feet (150 metres) at the slow rate associated with this spreading out, especially when there are stronger thermals around at a lower altitude, I have found from my own experience that it generally does pay to do so at the end of a soaring day. At that time of the day one is often flying for survival rather than for high average speed and any thermal is better than nothing at all. In addition, the large areas of slowly rising air in the upper band of the convective layer can be easily used to improve the achieved glide angle, without in any way spoiling your average speed – on the contrary, they will improve your overall speed by minimising the need to stop and climb. Another reason for staying high at the end of the day is that at that late hour blue thermals are better organised at height and easier to use than those low down.

Opposite – climbing away after a winch launch

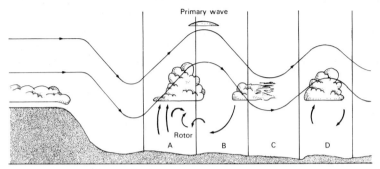

Figure 5.   Wave flow influence on convection

Wave effects on thermals

Local soaring in wave can provide useful background experience for subsequent cross-country flights. In the context of cross-country and competition flights based on thermal lift the use of wave in itself is, in my experience, seldom of any real advantage, but I find it very useful to both appreciate and understand the influence of wave on the structure of thermals as well as on their distribution. In the next few paragraphs I will concentrate, therefore, on the influence of wave on thermals, and give only brief thoughts on wave flying proper.

Wave above the convective layer can have a startling effect on thermals below. It can both enhance thermal strengths in places and dampen them down in others; also, in such conditions thermal strengths cannot always be assessed accurately from the appearance of the cumulus clouds, which may be misleading.

Figure 5 illustrates a simplified wave flow pattern and in the text following I will discuss the wave's likely influence at selected points.

At A the upwards flow induced by the wave will be felt in the lower levels of the convective layer. Even when the wave effect is weak, thermals in this region will be both induced and made stronger and as a result unusually high rates of climb can be found compared with those normally achieved on that day. Any cumulus clouds associated with thermals in this area will grow rapidly but the best lift will invariably be slightly into wind of the main cloud mass and, frequently, will be in the blue upwind of the cloud.

When gliding in these conditions you will find that as you climb in the thermal the wind will carry you further across the wave until by the time you reach cloud base you will be directly below the leading edge of the cumulus cloud. Clearly, to maintain good thermal conditions you will need to edge into wind continually so as to avoid being drifted into the down-going part of the wave flow.

At B cumulus cloud is still present, though decaying, and the descending wave is dampening thermal activity, often to near zero. Of all regions, this is by far the most frustrating when flying in thermals influenced by wave. From low down the cloud often looks quite usable and yet the wave will have largely destroyed the convection, which leaves you with the problem of how to realise some order out of this difficult situation. The answers are twofold, I believe; you either stay high in which case the clouds will produce lift for a time, or, if you are low down, you turn either into wind or downwind in order to contact the thermals induced at A or between C and D.

It is common to see lenticular-like medium or upper cloud above the area between A and B and, while this may be a good indicator of the conditions in the convective layer, it cannot be relied upon to indicate the positioning of the thermals below which have been influenced by wave. The wave pattern well below the lenticular cloud may be different from that higher up. What such clouds do indicate, however, is the presence of wave generally and they should encourage the pilot to analyse the air mass to ascertain the effect of the wave on his level of the atmosphere. Once again, an air mass read-out on the variometer will help you to work out what is really happening.

At C is the characteristic gap between wave crests which is normally marked in the convective layer by a lack of cloud; thermals in this region will often be weak. Those forming to the left of C, under the downgoing part of the wave, will show an initial strength which would normally indicate a good thermal, but the rate of climb will fall off rapidly as the thermal is dampened by the wave. Under these conditions you will repeatedly find thermals being cut off whilst they are still well below the level of convective cloud base nearby. It is frustrating to fly in these conditions but understanding the influence of wave will better enable you to move away from the sinking air and into the ascending part of the wave.

Wave above the convective layer can have a strong effect on thermals below – photo from rear cockpit of Janus

At D we have an area of slight wave influence where thermals will be enhanced but, by reason of the reduction in vertical velocity of the wave, its influence will not be as significant as at A. The reduction in vertical velocity will normally continue the further you move downwind from the wave trigger until eventually the thermals and cumulus will behave in the expected way. This will not always be the case, however, as weather conditions conducive to wave can often cause large scale wave motion which can cover the whole of your operating area, and it is not uncommon for the visible signs of this activity to be inconspicuous from the heights at which thermal soaring is conducted. Clearly, this demands caution and concentration if the soaring flight is to be successful.

The general characteristic to watch for under such wave influenced thermal conditions is a marked degree of turbulence in the convective layer, especially in the area influenced by the upwards wave motion. Thermals will tend to be very narrow and they will change their structure continuously, so that a glider has to be almost continually re-centred in the core. As I have already mentioned, thermals off the same general area of terrain will drift into the down-going part of the wave. As a result you will have to keep adjusting your circling so that you maintain the same position over the ground and thus keep in the best position in relation to the wave. If you fail to do this then you will soon be in the area influenced by the down-going wave and, if you are not careful, you will soon find yourself on the ground.

We have looked at some aspects of thermal recognition, but I believe the most effective way of developing this ability is to fly under as wide a variety of weather conditions as possible and to learn as much as you can from the experience. There is no substitute for this and there is no magic, instant, written solution. Resist, at all costs, therefore, the temptation to fly just on the good days. You must do all you possibly can to fly whenever practical, as only by doing so will you encounter the complete spectrum of soaring conditions to be found on cross-country flights.

IMPROVING YOUR TECHNIQUE

For the budding cross-country and competition pilot the potential for developing cross-country and racing techniques during local flights is immense. Once you have mastered the basics of soaring and once you have achieved confidence and consistency in your approaches and landings you should begin to refine your skills. Particular areas for attention are thermal entry and exit; if appropriate, flying with water ballast; hill soaring and, although it is not permitted in all countries, cloud flying. I will discuss each of these and suggest points you should concentrate on in order to make the best possible use of your local flights as a prelude to cross-country flying.

Longer flights

Since most cross-country flights involve several hours of flying time it is important to devote some attention to local practice flights which also last several hours. In club flying the practical problems of obtaining a machine for that amount of time may mean that you can't train extensively in this area, but even so, I believe it is fundamental to successful cross-country flying to have experienced the problems of soaring and concentrating whilst suffering a measure of fatigue. To launch off across country without having such experience is to risk inefficient soaring towards the end of the flight, and, far worse, it produces the potential problem of an away-landing whilst tired. Better to have practised all this within the safety of gliding range of your home airfield than to learn the hard way with a broken glider.

Perhaps the best thing you can do to help is to ensure, as far as possible, that you fly your five hour duration flight for your Silver C before you make any attempt to fly cross-country. This will at least ensure that you have one long flight to your credit, but you should aim to do more than this if you can.

Thermal entry

You should aim to develop your skill in entering a thermal cleanly and centring correctly within the first turn. This is highly important, as time spent attempting to centre will seriously degrade your achieved rate of climb. You may find it surprising to learn that, as a general rule, your average rate of climb is often only half of that indicated on the variometer. The 'loss' is due to the time taken to establish the climb and the time taken to exit at the top, during which the glider may not be climbing at all. You will be able to observe this yourself if you get a chance to fly in a glider equipped with a rate of climb 'averager'; the averager can be started at the moment the glider is decelerated in the thermal and stopped as it leaves. The results will give a clear indication of your thermalling efficiency, and practice will show you clear improvements. Should you have a chance to fly a glider equipped with this device I strongly suggest that you grab the opportunity as it will enable you to see clearly how only small errors in your technique can have a disproportionate effect on your achievements.

If you are joining a thermal which already has another glider in it you must take special care to maintain adequate lateral and vertical separation at all times. Don't fly close to other gliders until you have enough experience to do so. In particular, remember that the glider you are flying can gain several hundred feet during a zoom climb from cruising speed. This means that a glider which is initially well above you as you enter may be a potential collision risk after your zoom. So, watch it!

When learning the best way to establish yourself in a thermal you must first recognise the feel of it from the general turbulence

14

of the surrounding air; often your first indication of an adjacent thermal is given by this turbulence and not by any instrument indication. Your main concern is to determine how long after the initial turbulence and subsequent indications of lift on the vario-meter you should initiate your turn to centre in the thermal. With practice you will appreciate the delay between the onset of initial turbulence around the thermal and entry into the main core itself. Fortunately, thermal cores generally have a markedly firm feel and give a positive vertical acceleration on entry – a feeling well recognised by the human backside. Initiating your turn so as to achieve an accurately positioned circle will take much practice; sometimes you will need to roll into the turn as soon as you hit the core and on other occasions you will need to delay for a few seconds. The main factors affecting this delay are the thermal size and your own speed, which is why I suggest that you should practise the entry into thermals under a wide variety of weather conditions and from different cruising speeds.

The variometer has a fundamental part to play in assisting a clean thermal entry, and a good instrument with accurate total energy can take much of the 'guesstimation' out of the exercise. Of all factors affecting thermal entry, I am certain that good total energy is by far the most important and it is the one facet of instrumentation you must get absolutely right; there are no half measures in this respect. A good total energy probe will transform previously errant variometer indications into something which makes sense.

A further factor affecting thermal entry is the variometer performance itself. You should ensure, as far as possible, that the instrument gives a dead-beat response with only a short time delay in its indication. You should be certain that the installation does not react excessively to gusts because such conditions can be extremely misleading. The use of restrictors, filters and such like may be necessary. However, whatever variometer installation you are using, you should aim to become completely familiar with it as only by doing so can you begin to appreciate the nature of each individual thermal. Unfortunately, this means that you will often learn best if you confine your flying to just one glider so that you get thoroughly used to its variometer.

Pull-ups

On entering an area of lift you should reduce the speed of the glider to the appropriate figure for the prevailing conditions given by the variometer speed ring. When slowing down in these circumstances you should take care not to pull so hard that you can feel the 'g' force increase. To do so increases the lift demanded from the wing, and, hence, increases the induced drag to such an extent that your height gained in the zoom is noticeably reduced. Instead, a gentle but sustained pull-up is more efficient, but remember that you will need to begin lowering the nose before the indicated air speed has fallen below your intended flying speed. If you fail to do this you may find yourself with too low a speed for control and manoeuvre, although I hasten to add that there is no problem in flying below stalling speed providing you do not demand more angle of attack from the wings than the stalling angle. This, and the whole question of pull-ups and Dolphin flying, will be considered in more detail in later chapters.

Thermal exit

An efficient exit from a thermal can make a significant contribution to your overall performance. You can readily develop your skills in this respect during local flying and the practice alone can do much to improve your thermalling discipline. There are two particular points to watch: first, you should discipline yourself to leave the thermal when the rate of climb has fallen below the norm for the day, bearing in mind conditions en route and ahead, and second, you should ensure you do not lose height unnecessarily as you leave the thermal.

The first point, leaving the thermal at the right moment, can be covered by a rule of thumb and I suggest that when your indicated rate of climb has fallen to two-thirds or less of the norm for the day you should be on your way. You should, however, be prepared to stay with the lift if conditions ahead look doubtful, as you may well need the extra height in order to avoid reaching the ground before the next thermal. This can really only be learnt from experience and must always remain a matter of judgement. The technique for leaving the thermal efficiently is more straight-forward and involves only a simple appreciation of the well-known

Flying the ridge at Syerston above the River Trent

fundamental that you should reduce speed when in lift and increase it in sink. Add to this the fact that height losses will be excessive if you attempt to accelerate the glider from circling speed whilst you are in sinking air, and you will see that you need to establish cruising speed before you encounter the sinking air which surrounds any thermal. Judging when to accelerate is also something learned from experience: you must take conditions at the time into account, and take note of the proximity of other gliders in the thermal. What you should aim to do is to leave the acceleration until the last possible moment, such that you gain maximum benefit from the lift and yet achieve cruising speed just before you encounter the sink. If, however, the sink around thermals on the day in question is particularly strong then you will find it worthwhile to accelerate a little earlier and to plan to exit at a higher speed than normal, slowing down to the correct speed to fly for the thermal conditions, as given by the variometer speed ring, once you are completely clear of the area of sink around the thermal.

Hill soaring

The ability to hill soar can make the difference between completing a cross-country flight and making an outlanding. It is one of the basic skills of the accomplished pilot and is one which should be sought after by anyone of cross-country standard. On the other hand, because it involves flying low and fairly slowly, it is an area of flight which can be fraught with danger for the unwary and it is not an exercise to be attempted without first having had formal instruction. I will not dwell on the mechanics of hill soaring or on the basic techniques, but will concentrate on those aspects relevant to cross-country gliding.

Hill soaring, whilst flying cross-country, should be regarded as an emergency means of staying airborne under conditions which would otherwise result in an outlanding, in the belief that whilst you are still airborne there is a chance of completing the planned flight. I have used the technique successfully on a number of occasions, but equally, there have been times when hill soaring merely prolonged the agony with the eventual landing being no further along track than would have happened if I had made a straight glide out from the last thermal. But you win some and you lose some and, on balance, staying airborne is the best bet.

Practice in hill soaring can best be had by flying with a club based on or adjacent to a suitable hill, or by joining a formal expedition of your own club to a hill site. You should aim to be competent at soaring the hill under a wide variety of wind speeds and directions and under varied thermic conditions so that the basic skills become second nature. Above all, when hill soaring during cross-country flying, you should concentrate on learning how to contact thermals low down and then working up sufficient height in them for normal thermal soaring to be resumed, so that any cross-country flight could be continued. This technique of getting away from the hill demands particular skills because thermals triggered by the hill normally form minor streets which die a short distance downwind of the slope, which means frequent adjustments to the glider's thermalling turns are necessary in order to keep the machine towards the windward end of the thermal street. Figure 6 illustrates this point. The technique is similar to that used with wave-induced thermals except that the low height normally used for hill soaring, together with the rough terrain associated with hills, exacerbates the risks involved in getting downwind of the hill lift when low. In such cases it may prove impossible to regain the safety of the hill lift if you have failed to establish adequate height in the thermal, and have drifted too far downwind.

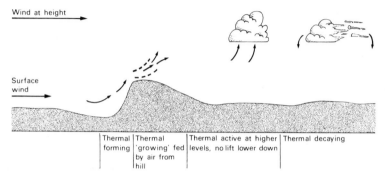

Wind at height

Surface wind

| Thermal forming | Thermal 'growing' fed by air from hill | Thermal active at higher levels, no lift lower down | Thermal decaying |

Figure 6.   Using thermals when hill soaring

Once you have mastered the techniques for using the hill and for contacting thermals off it successfully you should then develop your skills by gliding into the hill lift from several miles away, aiming to arrive at relatively low heights. This will simulate the type of conditions you could encounter later in your soaring experience when you resort to hill lift during cross-country flying. Naturally, for such practice it is best to use a site with the landing field at the bottom; it is not safe to arrive low over the top of the hill, and, having failed to contact lift, to then complete a landing on the top. Low approaches are dangerous at all times; they can be especially so when landing at some hill sites.

Cloud flying

Cloud flying can sometimes assist your cross-country flying but, with modern glass-fibre machines with sensitive aerofoils, the gains in height from cloud flying are often cancelled out by the loss in performance brought about by water droplets or ice accretion on the wing. I will, therefore, confine my advice to what you should consider before attempting to cloud fly and emphasise some of the points to concentrate on when developing your cloud flying skills.

When local flying, whether you fly in cloud at all depends on the national and local regulations. Where it is permitted, however, you should decide whether cloud flying will be helpful every time you have occasion to practice it during a cross-country flight. The main considerations are:

a   Can I glide to the next thermal safely, without climbing in cloud first?

b   What is the freezing level, above which it will pay not to climb?

c   What is the wind velocity at cloud flying altitudes?

d   Is the cloud I plan to enter the best one available to me?

Considering each point in turn, you should think along the following lines. If the answer to **a** is 'yes' then the only reason in favour of cloud flying is the potential for rapid climb and the subsequent long cruise. However, from my own experience, I have seldom found I have done better by cloud flying than my colleagues who stayed below cloud under the weather conditions I have indicated. I think the losses in aerodynamic performance, and in one's own flying efficiency, once blind, offset the potential gains. So, in general, stay out of cloud on days when cloud base and thermal distribution makes it straightforward to complete the flight in the clear.

The freezing level is obviously highly significant and largely dictates the height above which it will pay not to climb. Under these conditions you must discipline yourself to climb only as high as this and then you must level your wings and leave. Although this sounds easy I personally find it hard to do, simply because the rate of climb is often so high in cloud that it is hard to drag yourself away from it whilst the variometer is jammed on the stops. A word of caution; the latent heat of condensation within the cloud will raise the local freezing level by several hundred feet and, if you leave the cloud just above the freezing level but still free of ice, you may well find that the water droplets on the machine will freeze as soon as you fly into the slightly colder surrounding air.

A further consideration when deciding whether to cloud fly is the height of the freezing level in relation to the ground. In Britain, particularly in the Spring, this factor can assume great significance, with the freezing level being so near the ground that any ice accretion from cloud flying may not melt until the glider is back at ground level. A glider with ice on does not soar at all well, and so, having picked up ice, you may find yourself dragged inexorably to earth before it has had a chance to thaw. Even more frustrating, however, is the situation with a freezing level at around 1500 feet (500 metres) above ground level; in this event the ice will begin to clear the wings by about 1000 feet (300 metres) but a further 500 feet (150 metres) or so will be required for a complete thaw to take place, by which time it may be too late to establish contact with and start a climb in a thermal.

The third point, wind velocity at height, is absolutely funda-mental, and failure to determine its value can have potentially disastrous results. I certainly know of two cases in Britain where pilots have climbed high in storm clouds, during which they drifted out to sea, and from which they each only succeeded in regaining the coast at low altitude. In both cases, the pilots were unaware that the winds aloft were in the order of 100 knots. The lesson is obvious, and its application to cloud flying anywhere is equally important: whilst flying blind in cloud winds can drift you off course or into prohibited airspace unknowingly. So you must determine the wind velocity at the heights at which you will be operating and then note the total time you spend in the cloud. Wind speed multiplied by the time will give you the expected drift in distance over the ground. However, make sure that you appreciate the convention for describing wind direction. When we speak of a westerly wind, for example, we are referring to a wind *from* the west, which produces a drift *to* the east. In other words, a wind from 270° will cause a drift of 90°, which is the reciprocal bearing.

The final points to consider are the merits of the selected cloud itself. You should remember that the normal reason for cloud flying is either to maximise your chances of crossing a difficult patch of weather, or, in the context of cross-country flying, to improve your average speed. You should, therefore, be highly selective in your choice of clouds. If your aim is to transit an area of 'dead' air you should determine what height you need to climb to in order to achieve this and then select a 'growing' cloud near the edge of the dead area. Thinking for a moment specifically of cross-country flying, be fully prepared to divert off track in order to contact a suitable cloud; the extra distance flown will be of little significance if the achieved rate of climb is good.

A 'growing' cloud also tends to satisfy the second potential reason for cloud flying, that is, the expectation of a high rate of climb so as to justify a fast cruising speed with the consequent high average speed. It will also give less icing than an older cloud. The important thing in all this is not to be too hasty by soaring up into the first cloud you come across – rather, consider the options fully before you act. Once again, local flying is the time to try all this out – but take heed of the relevant regulations.

Water ballast

Flying with water ballast presents some variations in handling qualities. These are best discovered whilst flying locally rather than on a cross-country flight because the differences can be most marked. The two most noticeable effects are a reduction in rate of roll and an increase in stalling speed, both of which can produce problems for the unwary. The rate of roll problem is simply a question of increased inertia about the rolling axis, due to the weight in the wings, versus a roughly constant aileron power. The glider, therefore, takes longer than normal to complete any rolling maneouvre, and this relatively sluggish aileron response must be anticipated throughout the flight, especially when manoeuvring near to other gliders, as in a thermal. The other main effect, the increase in stalling speed, is only significant when thermalling and when approaching to land. In a thermal the glider will clearly indicate to the pilot that it needs to fly faster and the important thing is to let it do so. This extra speed will, incidentally, enhance aileron response and help to overcome some of the effects of the increased inertia in roll.

On the approach and landing the problem is a little more involved. First, it is normal practice to jettison your water ballast before landing but you must establish beforehand how long your particular load of ballast will take to jettison since you need to allow for this

Opposite – an ASW 20 being filled with water

time if you release it immediately prior to landing. In the event of an out-landing you will normally have jettisoned it much earlier, probably at the first sign of seriously deteriorating conditions if, like me, your courage is none too great when the weather turns sour. However, there are times when you will find yourself landing with a full load of ballast – indeed the later generations of GRP gliders are certificated for just this eventuality. If this happens, you must remember the increased stalling speed, say five knots in most instances, and you must increase your approach speed accordingly. This higher speed, however, presents a problem of energy dissipation after landing which, coupled with the greater weight of the glider, leads to a dramatic increase in landing roll and is a task which will defeat most glider wheel-brakes. Add to this the fact that the heavier the glider, the shallower the approach angle will be with any given combination of speed and airbrake setting, and you will appreciate that caution is the order of the day for heavy-weight landings. Particular caution is necessary, also, if you find yourself having to make a heavy-weight landing away from an airfield, shallow approach, higher speed, and longer roll-out being the main considerations here. If the ground is rough then your glider will stand some risk of being damaged. The moral is clear; drop your water ballast at least five minutes before landing.

Approach and landing

Landing in fields is a demanding exercise at the best of times and is not the occasion for improving your basic approach and landing technique. Naturally it follows that your local flying practice should include plenty of approaches under a wide variety of weather conditions. The pilots who confine themselves to having a few aero-tows and long soaring flights each summer are asking for trouble when the inevitable out-landing crops up. They will probably be less experienced than they think, will lack skill and basic judgement of approaches and they will not be able to cope with the situation. I believe it is fundamental that if you are to be a good, safe cross-country pilot you need plenty of recent experience at nothing more exciting than good old circuits! In this respect the wire launch probably gives the best value for money, but, regardless of how you do it, the point is that you must not limit your flying only to the good days when long flights and few landings are in order. You must, at times, reverse this and seek landings rather than hours. You should also seek to practise approaches under varied weather conditions and from varied positions in the circuit. Spot landings every time should be the rule and not the exception. Until you can do this you should not even consider flying beyond the gliding range of your base airfield.

The Bronze Badge awarded by the British Gliding Association recognises, among other things, a pilot's ability to perform an away landing. The fact that a pilot once passed the test is only an indication that the tester considered him safe to conduct an away landing at that time, and in no way does it exonerate the pilot from the need to develop his basic skills at precision approaches and landings. Once again, local flying is the time to do this.

Navigation

Soaring skills are a vital part of competitive success but navigation is of equal concern to the cross-country pilot. It is well worth appreciating that much useful practice can be obtained whilst local flying. The first skill to learn is that of orientation – knowing where you are and where you are pointing, and the first objective, therefore, is that when flying you should know at all times where the home airfield is in relation to you. You should aim not only to know which magnetic heading you will need to fly in order to reach the airfield, but you should know at any instant where the airfield is in relation to you in the cockpit – is it behind you, or to your left, right, and so on. Development of orientation is, in my view, a fundamental requirement for successful soaring and cross-country flying as it will make navigation simpler once you actually break the bonds of soaring locally.

The basic skills of orientation can be learned on the ground by careful study of a map covering your local flying area. Significant features within a few miles of the base airfield should be noted and related in direction to each other, and, whilst visualising yourself flying over a particular point in a chosen direction, you should work out where the airfield would be in relation to you at that time. The exercise can be repeated almost indefinitely until you really feel you know the area as fully as you can without actually flying over it. This exercise can also be repeated for areas further afield from base, in which case it will be useful to note those features you would fly over on your return track. Whilst practising this exercise it will be a good idea to develop the habit of turning the map in the direction in which you simulate the glider to be pointing. For example, if you are simulating a westerly heading then you should turn the map so that west is at the top, and likewise for other headings. (In the air this practice can considerably aid recognition of features because they will appear on the map as they do from the cockpit.) As you learn to orientate yourself mentally you should begin to associate a given position on the map with the magnetic heading required for successful flight from that point back to base, and you should repeat this for a whole variety of different locations.

Before taking off ensure that you have your map folded so that the part covering your local flying area will be clearly visible without further folding or unfolding. You will also find it useful to get into the habit of placing it in the cockpit so that when you pick it up your local area is on the side facing you. Also try to ensure that you have North at the top of the map each time you pick it up as this will give you a known starting point for the subsequent orientation of the map.

As far as possible, decide before you take off which features you wish to look at from the air and on the early flights concentrate on these features only, so that, once airborne and soaring comfortably, they can be searched out and related to the map without difficulty. Many features will look quite different when seen from above and you should, therefore, make a special mental note of any apparent differences. The air exercise should follow the same pattern as the simulated navigation and orientation exercise you conducted on the ground, but it will obviously take many flights to complete. One note of caution, however; because of the blind spot immediately underneath the glider, there is a natural tendency to assume that a feature just out to one side is, near enough, underneath, when in fact it may be a mile or so away.

When you have been cleared by your instructor of CFI to fly away from the home airfield, and only then, you should practise the basic orientation exercise further away at a distance of ten nautical miles (twenty km) or so. On these flights you should not only make a point of working out the magnetic heading you would need to fly to reach home from a number of different places, but you should relate it to what you can actually see to be correct. This will show up any errors in your assessment of the required headings.

26

As your ability to orientate yourself and to make use of the map increases, you will become more confident in flying at greater ranges from the airfield. We will return to some fundamentals of map reading later.

In these early exercises you should always aim to conduct your local flying at a height which takes account of both the wind and your distance from home, so that a straight glide back would get you overhead the airfield at an absolute minimum of 1500 feet (500 metres), although I recommend 2000 feet (600 metres) as being more suitable. Practise using a glide calculator on the ground until to do so is second nature; personally, I use the JSW calculator, manufactured by John Williamson, which is easy to use and unambiguous. I suggest you work your calculations using the cruising speed appropriate to the thermal strength as this has two main advantages. First, it will get you used to the idea of racing final glides, which you will use later on, because these involve the cruising speed principle. Second, it will give you a potential margin of height which you can realise by simply reducing speed by, say, ten knots thereby achieving less height-loss for the glide. I suggest you continue to use a substantial safety margin of height on all glides back to the airfield; the low final glide is something which only comes when you have reached competition standard and, even then, should be approached with great caution. Until that time it will be wise to keep these glides to a height above that at which you would normally select a field for an out-landing, for the simple reason that you would need this height should such a landing become necessary from the final glide. I stress once again, however, that you should never allow yourself to get into a situation where this might be possible until you have been cleared to fly away from the home airfield by your instructor or CFI.

In this chapter I have, I hope, focussed your attention on the things which I believe are essential to the success of the budding soaring pilot. There are no short cuts. You should concentrate on learning thoroughly the basic skills of pure flying and soaring before you consider venturing beyond the confines of your local area. Remember – 'fools rush in where angels fear to tread'!

Ready for take-off – a pre-production Nimbus 3

2
Barograph charts

You can learn a great deal about your soaring technique from a study of barograph traces of your soaring flights, an activity easily conducted from the comfort of your armchair at home. Time spent analysing your gliding and thinking about it objectively is time very well spent. This short chapter encourages you to do just that.

The barograph, in recording height against time, will help you assess your performance in two ways: the slopes of the vertical traces will give you a measure of achieved rates of climb and sink, and the saw tooth pattern of the trace gives you an idea of the quality of your soaring technique.

On a day offering uniform soaring conditions you should aim to achieve a barograph trace showing the up-slopes, which depict the climbs, as parallel lines. A gentle slope will indicate that you experienced a low rate of climb as a result of using a weak thermal, or perhaps because of poor flying technique in an otherwise respectable thermal. Conversely, a steep slope is indicative of a fast rate of climb. Using a calibration chart you can measure the rates; you may well find that the real rates of climb achieved are much less than you would think. Excessive variation in the slope of the lines is something you should try and avoid as it indicates that you were not critical enough in your selection of thermals – you probably accepted a wide variation in strengths. This raises the question of where the stronger thermals were – those of similar strength to the thermals which gave you your best rates of climb. The odds are that they were around somewhere and that you failed to find them, perhaps because you placed too much emphasis on staying high, and so had to use weaker thermals than was strictly necessary. This may sound simplistic, and you may well have had to use the weaker one in order to regain a satisfactory altitude, but the basic discipline of good soaring and reliable cross-country and, ultimately, competition flying is to strive for and search out the highest possible rates of climb as a matter of routine. The more time you spend circling, the longer the flight will take; in extreme cases excessive time spent in weak thermals on a cross-country flight can so reduce your average speed that you run out of daylight, thermals and ideas and finish up with an out-landing.

To highlight many of these points and to give you some useful ideas for analysing barograph records in more detail we will now examine a fictitious trace (Figure 7).

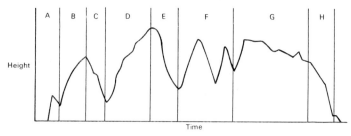

Figure 7.   Barograph trace (fictitious – for illustrative purposes only)

Section A

Section A shows the tow release and descent prior to contacting the first thermal. One point to note here is that for flights requiring barograph evidence, such as badge qualifying height gains, it is wise to ensure a small descent prior to your initial climb as this leaves a nick on the trace which is the datum for subsequent measurement.

Section B

Section B depicts the first thermal used and shows a good initial rate of climb but with a marked reduction at the top. You can take this to indicate, in all probability, that the thermal was either decaying, or the flying was poor and the glider was not held in the core of the thermal. You should have discarded the thermal (subject, of course, to being at such a height that you would reach the next thermal without great difficulty) or you should have improved your flying technique so as to maintain your rate of climb. Second-rate thermal flying is a bad habit which, if allowed to persist, will engender a sloppy attitude of mind and an overall poor performance at soaring. It will certainly not help you to win competitions.

Section C

Section C illustrates a fairly typical descent trace. The reduction in sink rate half-way down this part of the trace can often be evidence of the glider having flown close to a thermal, without making proper contact. Try to remember events as they actually happened and connect the visible record on the trace to the events in flight. Reduced sink may well be indicative of a neighbouring thermal and in such situations in flight it may be worth searching around for the thermal, especially when low down. Remember that thermals often travel up or near the same path, or drift off downwind from the same source and, in either case, it may be worth a detour, or even a temporary wait in weak lift, until something stronger appears. In this example given on the trace it is clear that the glider, in missing the nearby thermal, was forced to fly on and descend to a relatively low height before finding the next one, with the consequent increased risk of an out-landing.

Section D

Section D depicts a slow initial climb followed by a fairly fast but ragged climb with a slow climb at the very top. You can normally take this to indicate the initial climb to have been made on the edge of a strong thermal, contact eventually being established with the real thermal core. On the other hand, it could also be caused by a climb being flown in the remains of an older thermal with a fresh bubble then coming up the same path, thereafter producing the improved rate of climb. Either way the slow climb took too long and the barograph trace clearly shows the time consumed. The relatively quick but erratic climb rate in the middle part of the tracing is indicative of poor centring in the thermal; with more accurate flying the rate of climb would have been much better. The rapid fall off in the rate of climb towards the top of the thermal is clearly depicted and this should have been the signal to leave.

Remember the rule of thumb: two-thirds of the best rate of climb is the cue to leave. On the other hand, a slow climb at the very top can sometimes indicate your having flown through a neighbouring thermal during your exit from the previous one. Finally, it is worth noting that the fall-off in climb can also, at times, indicate that the thermal was reaching an inversion layer, with the consequent reduction in the rate of climb.

Section E

Section E depicts a higher than average rate of descent. In analysing this you could deduce correctly that it might have been caused entirely by flying at a higher speed than on the other descents and without any good reason. However, if this was not the case, then you must ask yourself whether you were flying in sinking air unnecessarily and, if so, then query whether you could have avoided so doing. Naturally it is advantageous to avoid such conditions but it is well nigh impossible to recognise them in flight unless the glider's variometer is capable of indicating what the air mass, rather than the glider, is doing. I firmly believe that this air mass facility is fundamental to really successful cross-country gliding as it enables sinking air to be recognised almost instantly. I would go so far as to say that it is almost as important a feature as proper total energy compensation. In your analysis of this part of the trace you will need to remind yourself of the options open to you when flying in sinking air; either you can increase speed to follow the 'speed to fly' indications, or, if you can do so in time and assuming you can work out where sink might be lurking, alter heading by about 30° so as to avoid the sink region altogether. This latter action will give you an across track speed (in still air) of fifty per cent of your true air speed for a reduction of only fourteen per cent in forward speed. When executing such a detour, it will pay, whenever possible, to alter heading so as to follow a route which takes advantage of closely spaced lift areas – in other words, following a route of maximum energy.

Section F

Section F depicts a classic pattern of a climb/cruise, typical of medium performance gliders. Notice that the rates of climb are consistent, indicating steady flying and a selective approach to thermals. It is also clear that the glide has been continued for a considerable time before the next thermal has been accepted. This practice, of itself, can often increase average cross-country speeds because it minimises time which is inevitably wasted every time the glider is decelerated and centred in a thermal; too many thermals give too great a loss overall. In addition, a long glide between each climb increases the number of thermals which are sampled and thereby raises the probability that a strong one can be selected and used. Remember this portion of Figure 7 and try to achieve something similar yourself.

Section G

Section G is fairly typical of the trace often produced by Dolphin style flight. By this technique the glider will have been flown at reduced speed in any lift encountered and under good conditions will have maintained more or less level flight. The main point to appreciate about this type of flying is that it only really works well when lift is plentiful and closely spaced, and even then its true value is only realised in very high performance machines. Under these conditions you should aim to produce such a trace yourself.

Section H

Section H shows a final glide in which the rate of descent was increased significantly about half-way down. When you see this on a barograph chart it can normally be taken to indicate that the glider was found to be above the required slope and that height was converted to speed in order to cross the finish at a fairly low height. Unfortunately the extra speed gained does not compensate for the additional time spent gaining the surplus height in the first place. Ideally, the final glide should be flown at the speed given by the rate of climb in the last thermal used and this should be borne in mind when analysing the final glide path shown on the barograph trace.

Assuming that the initial part of the final glide *was* flown at the correct speed for the prevailing thermal conditions, the height which would have been needed for the glide at this speed can be found by drawing a line from the point on the trace corresponding to the crossing of the finish line, parallel to the initial descent line. Where this line intersects the trace line of the last climb is the height at which the glider *could* have left for the final glide. You may consider that the height so given leaves little margin for error, but in reality this is not true; a good safety margin of height may be attained by reducing speed to a figure nearer to that needed for the best glide angle. Obviously, if the glide is to be made at a speed close to the best glide angle then extra height will be a wise precaution.

Analysis of various sections of a barograph trace is a thoroughly worthwhile exercise. For best results it should be completed as soon as possible after the flight so that the events are still clear in your mind, but it is also useful to look back at your older traces, which may well highlight persistent faults. It is also very helpful to compare your traces for a particular flight with those of another pilot who flew a similar flight on the same day. If the other pilot is more skilled than you are, you can learn a lot from him. It can even bring those foggy winter evenings to life!

3
Preparation for flight

'Do not assume – check!' is a well known expression amongst professional aviators. If you are to operate a glider effectively, and particularly if you aspire to competition successes, you should aim to match the standards of the professional. For reasons of safety alone you must be thorough in your checking of the aircraft and its systems and for competition work you must also be confident that your machine is fully serviceable. In this chapter we will examine just a few of the extra considerations you should automatically bear in mind if you are looking for success in competition.

Airframe

Clearly, the glider itself is fundamental to such success and naturally we must do everything possible to make sure it behaves as it should; checking the airframe makes a vital contribution to this. It is a relatively straightforward matter and is, of course, a routine check which is taught at the earliest stages of a glider pilot's career. With regard to competitive gliding the inspection and preparation of the glider before flight is particularly important and requires, I suggest, slightly different emphasis from that for local soaring. However, I must stress that for both situations the standards of 'airworthiness' should be the same and I am only going to suggest aspects of the inspection which, if neglected, would be more likely than others to produce problems on a competition flight.

In competitive flight the airframe is often exposed to the limits of its placard as regards speed. Any undue wear in the control system or main attachment points will make the aircraft susceptible to airframe oscillations in flight, with the attendant clunks and worrying sound effects, and ultimately more susceptible to flutter. This is not to say that flutter will result but that it could in extreme circumstances. Obviously, for any flight these aspects should be checked but, life being what it is, they tend to be overlooked in the context of routine club flying. Likewise, it is especially important to check the airframe for structural soundness and possible damage. To emphasise this I will just mention two examples. In the first case a 'T' tailed glider experienced serious tail flutter whilst crossing a finishing line at high speed and low altitude. It was potentially disastrous – observers saw the tailplane and fin oscillating laterally by up to 30°. The cause of the problem was a structural failure at the base of the fin arising from damage brought about by a previous ground-loop incident. The damage was not obvious from an exterior inspection of the skin but it would have been easy to determine it by checking the tailplane for the rigidity of its fitting. Had this been done the whole rear end of the fuselage would have been found to be noticeably more flexible than normal. I can recollect another incident in which damage to the tail region arising from a ground-loop *was* discovered by the pilot during his pre-flight inspection and possible disaster was thereby avoided. So check your glider thoroughly before flight each day, and also after any landing which isn't perfectly normal.

Instruments

The functioning of all instruments should be checked before flight. It is no use assuming that the systems are serviceable from a previous day's flying as all too often someone has fiddled with them and affected their proper functioning. You must get into the habit of paying particular attention to instruments as without them it is not possible to emulate modern standards of soaring flight.

The first instrument to consider is the air operated variometer. This type can be checked in a variety of ways but I prefer to squeeze lightly one of the air tubes which feed it (this should show a clear movement of the pointer). Alternatively, a very light puff of air blown past the total energy head will ascertain the basic functioning of the instrument by causing the pointer to flicker. It is not really practical, nor in my view is it necessary, to check quantitative variometer response on the ground.

Electric variometers have their own checks specified by the various manufacturers and I do not think it is practical to generalise as to what should be done. The one element common to all types,

Out on the launching grid – Mini-Nimbus, with pilot Dickie Feakes

however, is the electrical power supply which must be checked to see whether there is sufficient for your intended flight.

Airspeed indicators can be checked in various ways. With those driven from a 'pot-pitot' in the nose of the glider the easiest method is to press the palm of your hand against the nose orifice to increase the pressure inside so that a small indication is given by the instrument. Airspeed indicators, which are connected to pitot tubes protruding from the aircraft, can be checked by sealing the tube with a damp finger, and heating the tube itself with the hand. The air inside will be heated and the expansion will cause enough needle movement for you to see whether the indicator is working properly. A further method, which can be used with all installations, is to blow lightly across the orifice whilst a colleague checks for a flicker of the instrument needle. This should be carried out with great care as over-zealous blowing can cause excessive instrument indications and possible damage.

Airspeed indicators operated by pitots mounted coincidentally with a nose air intake are more difficult to check. The hand-heating method is impractical because of the poor access offered by this installation, and the palm of the hand technique is unlikely to work because air will leak away into the ventilation system. The most practical method is to first check the pitot-static connections for security and then to pinch the pipe from the pitot so as to increase the pressure between the pinched area and the air speed indicator. This should show a positive reading on the instrument.

Other instruments should also be checked for serviceability. If you intend to cloud fly, you should check the functioning of any blind flying instrument fitted. Of special importance is the checking of the turn needle to establish that it indicates correctly when the glider is yawed. Because the motor for this instrument is DC it will work equally well, but in the wrong sense, with the electrical supply connected in reverse. In a perfect world you should check battery voltage as well and I strongly recommend the fitting of a miniature voltmeter in the glider to facilitate this and, moreover, to enable you to monitor battery voltage whilst in flight. Finally, make sure that the compass works and that it indicates sensible headings. So many do not!

Barograph

Don't take the glider to the launching site until you have installed a serviceable and sealed barograph. It is important to get into this habit at the earliest stage of soaring because so often the achievement of even basic badge qualifying flights goes unrewarded for lack of suitable barograph evidence. Also, you can learn much from both a casual and a detailed examination of the barograph records of your soaring flights, as we discussed in the last chapter.

The particular point to bear in mind is that the barograph should be correctly sealed by or under the supervision of an observer recognised by the appropriate national agency for the FAI. The need for scrupulous care over this matter, and over all questions of barograph preparation, cannot be stressed too strongly as the opportunities for fraud are, regretfully, always present. On completion of a flight which might qualify for a badge or record the barograph should not be opened without reference to the observer, otherwise the barograph trace could be considered null and void.

Whilst considering barographs it will be worthwhile looking briefly at the mechanics of preparation and fixing of traces. The most common system, and in many ways the most foolproof, is that using smoked paper or foil. For blacking these I suggest you use solid camphor as your smoke producing agent in preference to the dirty oily wicks of paraffin burners which make such a mess of everything. Having affixed the paper or foil to the drum, place a chip of solid camphor on a flat wooden block and ignite it in a draught free atmosphere, inside the trailer for example. The burning camphor will give off a thick black smoke which is near perfect for blacking and will cover the drum in soot in only seconds. After flight, I prefer to use a hair spray for fixing the traces – but, caution! If the nozzle is held closer than six to eight inches from the drum you run the risk of 'spotting' the trace badly, or even of washing it off. My advice is to experiment on an unused part of the trace before spraying the bit that really matters.

Of course you can use an ink trace barograph which eliminates all this trouble. On the other hand, such a system is not always reliable at temperatures below freezing and, therefore, for high altitude flight, the smoke trace is probably a better bet. You can also use pressure sensitive paper on some barographs and this is a simple and reliable system which makes no mess and requires no fixing.

Maps

If the glider is to be flown more than a few miles from the airfield it is wise to ensure that a map is available. The map carried should be of a scale sufficient to enable you to pinpoint your position without difficulty and yet compact enough to carry conveniently. From my own experience I have found the 1:500,000 scale topographic to be the most practical for routine navigation over a whole variety of countryside in different parts of the world. However, when flying over well featured terrain, such as in Europe, I have found it very useful also to have a set of 1:250,000 prepared for the whole route. These more detailed maps are ideal for precise positioning, required in conditions of poor visibility and when determining your position should you have to make an out-landing. They are also most useful in helping over detailed positioning in the turning point photographic zone. They have the added advantage of being suitable for use on the road and, therefore they give you the opportunity of having the same map as your retrieve crew, which can sometimes be very helpful.

In certain parts of the world where the visibility is very good and where features are few, but are marked on the map, the 1:1,000,000 scale topographic can be entirely satisfactory for routine navigation.

Maps carried should be prepared so that, when folded, the base airfield will be at the centre of one of the exposed sections. Range circles should be drawn from the centre of the base airfield at ten nautical mile intervals (twenty kilometres will be a suitable metric near equivalent) out to about twenty miles. It will also be useful to have a self-adhesive compass card positioned over the base airfield, placed so that it is orientated to magnetic north. Track lines drawn from the airfield can then be read direct from the compass card in degrees magnetic which will equate with the glider's compass indication, providing that it has been accurately adjusted. Track lines drawn towards the airfield will be the reciprocal of the figure given at the point where the lines cross the card, that is, 180° different. Figure 8 illustrates the various additions to the map which I have suggested.

As for maps, on any flight likely to take the glider more than a

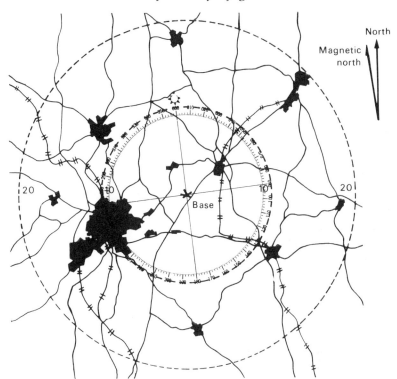

North

Magnetic
north

Figure 8.   Map: principle features to be added

few miles from the airfield it is wise to check that a glide calculator is carried. There are a variety of models produced but all you need to ensure is that the type carried is suitable for the performance of the glider you are flying.

Pilot welfare

Long flights inevitably raise the question of provision for urination. The ladies appear to have little problem, being blessed with a quite remarkable staying power. The men however, seem to have less self discipline than the fairer sex and may well have problems keeping comfortable in the air. Some form of relief system is therefore necessary but it is not so important what system you actually engineer, more it is a matter of being able to use the system in flight. This is often more difficult than imagined and can involve basic psychological inhibitions. Suffice to say, staying off the tea and coffee immediately before flight is perhaps the best way of easing the problem.

On an allied topic, do not forget to provide drinking water if you are planning a flight lasting more than two to three hours. In hot countries the water is crucial both for in-flight consumption and for use after an out-landing, but in Britain the need is less critical. I suggest that you develop the habit of carrying a half-litre sealed plastic container of water on all long flights. When in need of a drink, remove the lid slowly to allow pressure to equalise. A more sophisticated system involves fixing a bottle into the cockpit and providing an outlet through a plastic pipe. Two considerations arise here: the first is to ensure that the bottle is given a separate vent to avoid the cockpit being flooded every time the glider ascends, and the second is to arrange the plumbing so that water does not syphon out after you have taken a drink. This can easily be overcome by, either blowing back down the pipe after each use, which I am sure could be considered to be very vulgar, or by stowing the outlet from the pipe above the level of the water in the bottle. Both involve elementary plumbing well within the capabilities of every glider pilot!

Maintaining an adequate blood sugar level is important if you are to keep yourself at peak performance in the air and I suggest you carry sweets or glucose tablets with you in the cockpit. I personally prefer glucose as its beneficial effect seems to be almost immediate, but this is probably partly psychological and no doubt some doctors will shoot holes in my belief. However, I am sure that blood sugar plays an important part in coping with the physiological pressures of flight and it should not be overlooked.

Sunglasses are very useful as they can cut down glare and so help to reduce fatigue in flight. It is well worth buying a good quality pair, and my own preference is for the brown-tinted Polaroid type as they not only solve the problems of glare but help you recognise those clouds likely to be associated with good thermals. They can also help you perceive blue thermals, especially under hazy conditions.

A sun hat is essential in all weather conditions other than thick overcast. Too much sun on your head is undesirable at the best of times but in the air its effect can be exacerbated by height and by long flights. Also, because body movement is restricted, the sun tends to strike just one area of the head, and this can cause earlier onset of sunburn than you might normally expect. Sunburn can produce some very unpleasant effects (quite apart from a pink skin) which can seriously affect the ability to concentrate and fly safely. It is something to be treated with respect.

Whilst on the subject of clothing, it is worth considering other items of dress. The first thing to bear in mind is the likely temperature in the cockpit whilst in flight. At certain times of the year and in particular climates it will be cold whilst flying, especially if the sun is obscured by cloud, and so you will naturally need to wear suitable cold weather clothing, especially around the feet. The more common problem, though, is getting too hot whilst flying, with the canopy of the glider performing the function of a glasshouse; the danger here is in exposing too much of the body to sunlight and running the risk of sunburn. The simple rule is to keep the arms and legs covered. But in considering dress remember that it is not only conditions in the cockpit which you must take into account but also the environment in which you might find yourself if you have to land out on the flight. Sometimes this can involve a night in the glider whilst awaiting your crew and, as I know from experience, it gets very cold in the middle of the night, even in Britain in mid-summer.

Footwear also deserves a mention. It will be tempting to wear lightweight shoes for comfort whilst airborne but if you land out you may well have to walk a fair distance to civilisation. Always wear shoes which you can walk in as a first priority, and then try to ensure that they meet the 'comfort whilst flying' need as a second priority only. You only have to land once in a muddy field full of spiked thistles which you must walk over to get to the nearest telephone, to be convinced of the wisdom of this advice.

This brings us on to the question of survival when flying a glider cross-country. Remember that even parts of a highly populated country such as Britain can prove very inhospitable to the glider pilot after an unscheduled outlanding; consider then the scale of the problem if you happen to be flying over less populated landscapes and think of the consequences of an out-landing in such country. My advice is simple; always ensure you have sufficient water and food to enable you to stay alive in the event of an outlanding on the most inhospitable and inaccessible part of the

The author in his ASW 17 (*David Platt*)

countryside covered by your planned route. If you follow this rule you will not go far wrong. It is also a good idea to ensure that your survival pack of food and water is beyond your reach in flight, so that greed does not have the upper hand!

Depending on the conditions under which you are flying, you may need to consider other aspects of survival, such as space blankets, locator beacons and snake-bite kits.

Finally, there may well be many other items which you may feel should be considered and checked before a competition or even a straightforward task flight. The main point to grasp, however, is that for any flight it is essential to check the glider and its equipment and your own needs if you are to develop the methodical attitude so necessary for success.

4
Extended local flying

The boundary between local flying and the beginning of cross-country work is indeterminate and, in this book, is more for convenience than for any other reason.

Once you have developed both your basic skills and your confidence by flying locally you should begin to branch out into training yourself for cross-country flying by deliberately conducting flights away from your base airfield. However, let me stress once again that you should on no account stray beyond your local soaring area without the prior approval of your instructor. This chapter will concentrate on aspects of soaring which should lay a sound foundation, and eventually enable you to complete demanding cross-country flights.

Efficient flying

The first step, I suggest, is to develop your capacity for efficient flight. By efficient flying I mean not only the use of strong thermals but making a determined effort to avoid wasting time finding them and centring on their lift. 'Low loss' flying would be an apt description, and it is really only an extension of the sort of things you should have been doing previously on your local soaring flights.

The procedure I suggest you adopt is to make a mental note of the best sustained thermal of the day and thereafter during the flight try not to use thermals which do not come up to that same standard. Equally, you should, as far as is practical, stop using a thermal when its strength has fallen significantly below the best it has given and you will remember that I recommended that a reduction in indicated climb rate down to two-thirds of the norm for the day suggests it is time to leave. In adopting this practice you will find, initially, that you experience some long glides as you will,

45

perforce, pass many thermals of indifferent strength, which, although strong enough to climb in, are significantly below the standard you have set for the day. The difficult aspect to master is learning when to forsake the search for strong lift and accept something less good. But this is the advantage of conducting such training whilst fairly near to your base; if you overdo the drive for strong lift you merely have to chicken out and land back and then pay for a further launch. You will not need a retrieve!

To conduct this exercise successfully, I suggest the first thing to do is to have a good look at thermal conditions in the area of the desired line of flight and then make a conscious effort to select a precise route through the air, which appears to offer the most promising thermal conditions. Such a route will certainly not be a straight line. In other words you are seeking the path of maximum atmospheric energy, and, in my view, this is one of the most important concepts of cross-country gliding.

To put this into practice, as you fly along this route of maximum energy you should aim to glide at the MacCready speed indicated by your *achieved* rate of climb, this being the height gained divided by the total time spent in association with the thermal. (As a general rule, half the indicated rate of climb will be approximate to the achieved rate of climb.) Any lift found should be ignored, other than by slowing down in it in accordance with the speed ring indications, until either a thermal meeting your criterion for rate of climb is found or you reach the 'chicken' height at which prudence says 'to climb slowly is better than to land prematurely'. The precise height at which you do this will depend upon the weather conditions, your experience, your confidence, and, in the early exercises before you venture far from home, on your location in relation to the base airfield.

If the convective layer is deep the thermals will normally be wider apart than if convection is shallow. Thus, under deep convective conditions you will need to operate at a greater height than you would if thermal activity were confined to a more shallow layer. I suggest you use this fact as the basis for deciding what I have chosen to call the 'chicken' height, and until you become experienced enough to make a more flexible assessment I suggest you use a figure of one-third of the convective depth as this height. However, you will need to modify the selected height in the light of the terrain below and the resulting height needed to conduct a safe out-landing as well as by the context in which you conduct this training exercise, be it local soaring or more extended cross-country flying. Anyway, from this principle it follows that, for a 6000 feet (1800 metres) layer, 2000 feet (600 metres) above ground level would be the figure, which I am sure you will agree, is a reasonably conservative height. If, however, the depth of convection is only about 3000 feet (1000 metres), then the one-third rule gives only 1000 feet (300 metres) as the 'chicken' height and I consider this to be rather too low in relation to the out-landing requirement, assuming that the pilot is relatively inexperienced. In this case I feel that around 1500 feet (500 metres) would be a better height to use. If you are flying over mountainous terrain a whole series of additional safety factors must be included as well, but they will be dictated by local requirements and any generalisations here won't be sufficient.

The height chosen should not be regarded as a hard and fast distinction between flying for speed as opposed to flying for survival but, rather, it should be used as a guide only. For example, if at some height above your 'chicken' height it becomes clear that the air ahead of you is devoid of good lift then you should slow down immediately to a speed warranted by the conditions anticipated. Remember that, in the context of a continuing cross-country flight, the MacCready speed is not indicated so much by the strength of your last thermal but by the assumption that your next thermal will be of that same strength. Equally, if, as you reach 'chicken' height, you notice a good thermal about a mile ahead and you are confident that it will work, then you should pluck up your courage and glide on until you reach it. Just how far you can push in this way is a matter you can only learn from experience and, in competitions, it is often this capacity which separates the champion from the runner-up.

Mini out and returns

My next suggestion is actually an extension of the type of local soaring most pilots usually undertake. Instead of flying around your home airfield more or less at random, take advantage of the excellent opportunities you have in such flying to practise short sectors of a typical cross-country flight. Take a straight line from, say, five miles (ten kilometres) one side of the airfield to a point five miles or so the other side. Obviously the distance of the points from the airfield will depend on many factors, not least being the weather conditions and the type of glider being flown. However, having determined this line and decided upon its precise starting and finishing points, you can then practise flying from end to end of it in the shortest time possible, an exercise you can repeat several times on each flight. With that as the general idea, let us now look at some details.

Having been launched, you should first work your height up to the appropriate level for the weather conditions pertaining and then move out at safe altitude to your selected starting point. Once you have got into the correct position and you feel ready to go, fly to the other end of your chosen line using thermals as effectively as you can in the way that you should have practised in your earlier local flying. You should aim to start and finish the exercise at similar heights on each run along the line. It would not be realistic to fly the route in a steady descending glide as this would give you no encouragement to practise the vital techniques of thermal location and their use.

Once you have managed to complete several exercises you should then take an interest in working against the clock by recording the times taken for each flight along your chosen route. You should then compare these times against the thermal conditions pertaining, as with experience this will enable you to relate specific weather conditions to your probable soaring performance, and determine how easily and at what average speed any planned flight may be completed.

Flying along your chosen local route can usefully be repeated many times and can be modified to suit local conditions. It can also be used as a basis for further practice at final glides; with the airfield being half-way along the line, you can practise final glides to overhead base, with a safety height added, from each end of the line. This will give you additional practice at contacting thermals at relatively low heights whilst still flying within comfortable range of your base airfield circuit pattern. However, in practising this take special care not to infringe the circuit itself by getting in the way of gliders preparing to land.

Mini triangles

Once you have mastered the fundamentals of efficient flying along a specific route you should move on to flying mini-triangles. Flying triangles will also give you most useful practice in learning to appreciate the subtle differences in both the appearance of cumulus clouds and in the 'feel' of thermals which so often seems to happen on different legs of a triangle. They will also give you plenty of practice at rounding of turning points and taking photographs at those points.

A worthwhile mini-triangle can be planned by extending the Mini Out and Return idea, again using reference points about five miles (ten kilometres) from the airfield as your turning points, depending on the wind and the type of glider you are flying. They can be either equally spaced around the airfield, with the airfield being the centre of the triangle, or by using just two remote turning points, the airfield itself can form the third corner. Triangle A in Figure 9 primarily lends itself to practise at the soaring and turning point aspects of the exercise in a sort of endless triangle, whereas triangle B provides an opportunity for repeated practices at start line procedure with the chance to complete a final glide at the end of the flight. B is also representative in shape and in the number of turning points, of the larger type of triangle normally flown on task or competitive flights.

One of the first things you will notice when flying these triangles is the apparent difference in character between thermals encountered on each leg. The climb itself in the core of the thermal will be the same on each leg but the feel of the air around the thermal may

Figure 9.   Flying mini-triangles

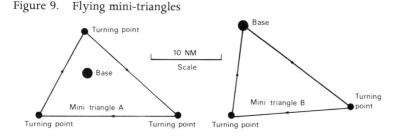

vary depending on the direction from which you enter it. This is because the motion within and around the thermal is, to some extent, dependent upon the wind, especially when the wind is strong. Likewise, the appearance of clouds varies, again depending upon which direction they are viewed from in relation to the sun and on some days the difference can be most marked. Both these points are ones which can often cause some difficulty and consternation shortly after a turning point has been rounded and the search for the next thermal is underway. As is so often the case, there is no easy way of learning other than by extensive practice and by keeping very alert whilst in the air. However, just realising that this problem is common to all pilots, and not just to you, will go a long way towards giving you the confidence to overcome these difficulties.

Turning point technique

For the best average speeds, turning points should be rounded as closely as possible to the vertically overhead position. This means that you need to learn a technique for combining a steep banking turn at the turning point with taking a photograph, as well as keeping a keen lookout for other gliders (turning points are potential collision areas). In looking at how we can best do this, the first thing to appreciate is that significant time can be saved by having the camera (I recommend two for reliability) mounted in fixed brackets so that the sightline between the pilot's eye and the wing-tip corresponds to the centreline of the camera frame. All that is then required at the turning point is to fly into the photographic zone, have a thoroughly good look-out for other gliders, and then bank to put the wing tip onto the point itself, hold the tip steady for a second or so to avoid blurred images and 'click, click' you should have the pictures in the bag. Success boils down to preparation and practice – isn't that always the case?

I recommend that the cameras you use have a 'cloudy/bright' setting because all too often turning points are under cloud-shadow, which can mean that a fixed aperture camera will produce indifferent negatives. Personally, I have two cameras fitted into the cockpit, with one normally set to 'bright' and the other to 'cloudy', and I have found that this gives a very good chance of

Rounding the turning point (the turning point is the L-shaped building)

producing technically satisfactory results. If you think you may be taking photographs under very poor light conditions then you will find it useful to consider carrying a 'used' flash cube or an electrical shorting device to place into the flash socket of cameras so equipped. On many inexpensive cameras the exposure is thereby increased and this can obviously be of use when light conditions are particularly bad. For example, it would be well worth adopting this trick on the last turning point on a very large task, which you are unlikely to complete because of the onset of dusk. Without it you may get no photograph, and a much reduced score.

Unless you are fully prepared, it can be very difficult to bank close to a turning point and produce a photograph which both portrays the required features, and is taken from the right position. Photographing the point itself, or a specific feature when this is required, is fairly easy if the wing tip aiming method I have already described is used. However, precise positioning in the photographic zone is the more difficult problem and demands extraordinary care if you are not to find that you have photographed the turning point from outside the specified photographic zone. The first thing you can do to alleviate the various difficulties is to draw the photographic zone accurately on your 'in use' map. Whilst it might be ideal to use a map of, say, 1:50,000 (approximately one inch to the mile), this may well be unmanageable in the cockpit and I suggest a compromise of 1:250,000. As we discussed in the last chapter, this is the scale of map you will need to have with you for some elements of navigation anyway.

You can use features on the ground to help you position yourself precisely in the photographic zone, and if you work this out beforehand, all you will need to do is to fly the glider to that spot to be sure of being in the zone. The thing to remember is that successful turning point photos begin with sound pre-flight planning, especially in determining the precise boundaries of the zone and its significant geographic features. Also, I think it worth saying that in competition flying the taking of crisp, clear pictures is more likely to endear you to the photo interpreter than blurred or badly aimed ones. You cannot afford to get on the wrong side of this particular contest official and so it is well worth the little extra trouble to get the pictures right first time.

Start line

A good start in top class competition flying can literally make the difference between winning and being runner-up. It is a detailed exercise in tactics, and is therefore an aspect of soaring which needs much practice if your subsequent cross-country racing performance is to be of potentially winning calibre.

Therefore, probably as the final step before starting full-blooded cross-country flying I suggest you practise start and finish line techniques.

The first thing to do is to decide upon a suitable start line, which I suggest is not orientated on the airfield for these early practice flights as this will keep you clear of the congested airspace in the immediate area of the airfield. For these early exercises I suggest you use a line feature on the ground as your start line in which case all you then need to do is to decide how long it is to be. To do this take a feature on the line to mark one end and then select another about half a mile (one kilometre) away along the same line. These two features can then be used to mark the ends of your start line. Next you should determine a suitable lead-in feature to the line, which in competitions is normally called the 'start-gate', and this, again, should be about one mile (two kilometres) from the line but at 90° to it. Figure 10 illustrates this point. Once your start line is defined you can go ahead and practise starts themselves.

The proximity of your pre-starting thermal to the start-gate, together with the maximum height of convection, has a significant bearing upon how you execute the practice start. What you should aim to achieve is a thermal within about one and a half miles (three kilometres) of the start-gate which will take you sufficiently high to enable you to then glide to the gate and arrive with enough height left over to be able to dive to a pre-determined speed for the

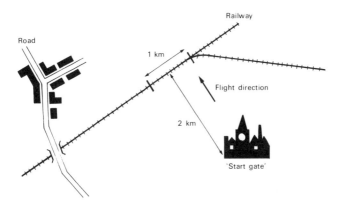

Figure 10.   Start line, for training purposes

line crossing. This means that in a Standard Class glider, for example, you should aim to be about 700 feet (200 metres) above the maximum start line height of 3281 feet (1000 metres) when you fly over the gate. If you then enter a moderate dive to gather speed you will be at about 100 knots (200 kph) and also at the maximum of 3281 feet when you cross over the line. However, this is a slight generalisation as, amongst other things, convective conditions near the start line itself can have a marked effect upon the height and speed you actually achieve at the line crossing. But at this stage, I think I have said enough, and I will leave discussion of some of the finer points until Chapter 6.

When practising starts it is particularly important to keep a very good look-out at all times. There will always be a number of other gliders in the area and this, together with the considerable speed differentials which will exist between your glider and the others which may be circling, makes the risk of collison significantly greater than normal.

To get the most practise in starts at this stage, I suggest you use the mini-triangle exercise as the method by which you will get the most opportunity to learn the fundamentals. First, I suggest you have a few practice runs at the mechanics of the start itself and, when you feel you have mastered the basic skills start thinking then about the soaring aspects relevant to the start. In other words, tackle the exercise in stages. It is well worth devoting substantial effort to getting your starting technique consistently right, particularly in arranging your start so that you run cleanly into good thermals immediately after the line crossing.

Whilst several factors need to be favourable if your start is to be of the best, the most important one is that the soaring conditions on-track beyond the start line must be suitable and must also be conveniently situated in relation to your intended track. This means that thermals marked by cloud, for example, should be in the growth rather than decay phase and should be positioned such that, allowing for the wind, they will be aligned with the track by the time you intercept them.

Basic final gliding

It is now time to mention the technique for completing a racing flight, with a final glide and crossing of a finish line. The scope for

Mini-Nimbus crossing a finish line

practising this aspect of gliding is extremely limited if your experience level is low. The difficulty with final glide practice is that it involves the need for a long glide in, say, from fifteen miles (thirty kilometres), if the practice is to be meaningful. I think you will appreciate that this could be at variance with the need to stay within safe gliding range of base, for the level of experience we have assumed. Also, meaningful practice will call for a line crossing at relatively low heights, say 500 feet (150 metres), and this will obviously conflict with routine airfield traffic. So, as I suggested earlier, you should confine your practice at this stage to familiarising yourself with the glide calculator and to doing the final glides with, say 2000 feet (600 metres) margin in hand. Later on, when you are cleared to fly cross-country, you can gradually bring the final glide heights down to whatever minimum pertains locally.

Detailed techniques for final gliding are discussed in Chapter 6, but it is appropriate to just mention briefly the main considerations, especially as they apply to mini-triangles.

The basic technique for a final glide is to calculate the height required from a given location so that the glide to the finish may be made at the cruising speed dictated by the rate of climb in the last thermal. You then glide from the height calculated at that same cruising speed, having added a few hundred feet safety margin. As each mile goes by you can read off from the altimeter the height left, together with your distance to go and then see how this compares with your original calculation. If you are ahead of the calculator, that is, you have more height than planned, then you may glide faster; if the opposite happens then you will need to slow down or even take more lift. This is really all you need to know at this stage.

Gaining confidence

As I have stressed so many times already, you should not venture out of gliding range of the airfield until you have been authorised to do so by your instructor. However, when you do become cleared to do so this does not, to my mind, mean that you should immediately rush off on your first cross-country. Rather, you should start by getting used to the feeling of being beyond gliding range of base and to staying airborne by your wits, knowing all the time that you have no friendly airfield below. In my view this psychological aspect is highly important – indeed, psychology, in as much as it affects confidence, is a major factor in cross-country flying.

Subject to local regulations and to suitable weather, I suggest you build up your confidence by gradually moving your local soaring and mini-triangles away from the airfield until you are working just beyond gliding range of it. Obviously this is not something you should do unless there are reliable soaring conditions to aid your return to base, but it can make a profound contribution to your subsequent success in completing planned cross-country flights. Eventually you will become so familiar with the sensation of relying wholly on your skill and judgement to keep you air-borne that your first cross-country will seem straightforward – as indeed it should be.

5
Your first cross-country flight

Your first cross-country is an important stage in your efforts to become an accomplished soaring pilot. It is an experience which should boost your confidence in your ability to soar and you should try to arrange the flight so that your chances of success are maximised.

To make such success as sure as possible I feel strongly that your first cross-country flight needs to be a straight line trip angled downwind to a goal, and preferably to a gliding site. This will give you the maximum chance of success whilst still providing adequate practice at soaring and navigation. As for the planned length of the flight, I suggest you aim for one of about thirty-five miles (sixty kilometres), as this will give you an adequate margin to allow for any reduction in effective distance flown arising from a large difference in height between that of tow release and landing. The rule laid down by the Fédération Aéronautique Internationale (FAI) is that the height of release above that of the landing must not exceed one per cent of the distance flown.

Assuming that the route you select follows the principles I have suggested above, this leaves the weather and the glider as the remaining factors bearing upon your success.

To consider the weather first, I believe it is more important to have straightforward uniform soaring conditions for your first cross-country, than to be able to reach any specified height above ground level before setting course. If the convection is deep then a much greater height will be needed before it is prudent to set sail from the airfield than if the convection is relatively shallow. In Great Britain a minimum height of 3000 feet (1000 metres) (above ground level) to be achieved before leaving for the cross-country is often laid down, but too rigid an adherence to this can lead to the failure of the flight. For example, on days with high cloud bases and

An ASW 20 in flight (*Paul Bolton*)

wide separation of thermals, 3000 feet may leave you insufficient time and opportunity to find the next thermal before you descend below the height at which you will need to select a field or suitable area for a possible outlanding. Equally, there are days when convection may be limited to, say, 3000 feet above ground level and in this case a departure height of 3000 feet is probably a little on the high side especially as thermals tend to be closely spaced under such conditions. In essence, you will need to adopt a flexible attitude of mind as to the minimum height required before departing cross-country. Bear in mind that you must always satisfy the requirement to have enough height to glide to the next likely thermal in order to arrive above the height at which you must choose a landing area.

The other main factor which can affect your chances of success is the glider itself but since your first cross-country flight will normally be done in a club or school glider, the machine you fly will be largely dictated by whatever is available. I believe that it is more important anyway that you should concentrate your efforts on flying your first cross-country in a machine whose handling and instrumentation you are completely familiar with, rather than trying to seek out and fly the highest performance glider available; glider performance alone does not ensure success. Moreover, your first cross-country is no time to start learning how to fly a strange machine.

Whilst it is absolutely essential to plan your flight as much as possible before you undertake it, your first cross-country will, to a certain extent, depend on opportunity. For a good chance of success, the weather will need to be near ideal with evenly spaced convection, light winds and with no excessive cloud development, but it is worth noting that compared with longer flights you will only require these conditions over a relatively small area. Such conditions can often be found during part of an otherwise mediocre soaring day.

We have already discussed some of the fundamentals of map preparation (Chapter 3) and there is no need here to do more than stress again the more significant points. The first step is to determine which destinations are suitable as goals, bearing in mind the various wind directions in your area which are compatible with cross-country flying. The choice of goals should be agreed with your instructor; your club will probably have several which are pre-planned and this will take care of the problem. However, I suggest you aim to have about six in number so as to allow for different winds. Having chosen your goals you should study them as much as possible so that, within reason, you know how they will appear from the air, what the local area will look like, and, also, the areas suitable for landing at the goals themselves.

To make it easier to see them on the map, it will be useful to highlight each of the possible goals. I think this is best done by drawing a small circle around each using a light coloured felt-tip pen; a pink or orange colour is probably the most effective, and the name of each place can be highlighted in the same way. It will also be helpful to stick a transparent plastic compass rose over your base airfield, if you have not already done so for your local flying exercises.

Having determined your goals, you should pre-plan your magnetic headings and write them in a convenient place on the white surround of the map so that they are readily available on the day you do your final planning and the flight itself. To remind you, magnetic headings are obtained by measuring the track required in relation to True North and then adding or subtracting for magnetic variation and for the deviation of the compass installation itself. The magnetic variation is found from the map and is added to the true track if it is west and subtracted if east. Compass deviation, alas, is generally not known in gliders because compass calibrations are carried out so infrequently, but when known it is applied in the same way as variation.

There is no need to draw a track line until you do your final planning on the day. Pre-drawn lines can lead to confusion in the air, and pilots *have* been known to follow the wrong one.

Once the weather promises to be suitable for the flight you can complete the planning by drawing a line from base to the destination which has been selected by your instructor. He will take account of all the relevant factors, such as airspace restrictions, weather, and such like. For your first cross-country the track chosen should normally be virtually downwind, as I have already suggested, and in this case there will be no need to allow for wind in your calculation of the heading required to reach the goal. However, should you ever have a cross-wind then, as a general rule, you will find that a heading allowance for wind of $2°$ per one knot of cross-wind component will suffice. This figure assumes an average speed of thirty knots (fifty-five kph): for sixty knots (one hundred and ten kph) speed the correction would be $1°$ per one knot of cross-wind component. At the risk of sounding simplistic, I must stress that the correction for cross-wind should have the effect of pointing the glider's nose into the wind. If you check this point each time you plan a flight you will avoid the common mistake of applying the correction in the wrong sense. You should note that this heading adjustment takes account of your anticipated drift off track whilst thermalling and, therefore, it is not the same as the adjustment which would be required to maintain track whilst in continuous straight flight at whatever cruising speed you might use. In this particular case the correction would be much less because your average speed in continuous cruising flight would be close to your indicated airspeed rather than the substantially lower figure common to gliding.

When you have completed this pre-flight planning you will be well advised to devote a few minutes to the study of the map. I suggest you make a mental note of the major features en route and at this stage of preparation you will find it useful to highlight the more prominent ones in the same way as you marked the goals earlier. In the air this will help you to concern yourself with the major pre-planned navigational features only, and will greatly ease the navigation itself. It will enable you to concentrate on flying and will help to prevent you from spending your time trying to navigate by reference to the small features either observed on the ground or noted on the map, as these can often serve to confuse you thoroughly.

Your preparation should include a briefing from your instructor which should cover the essential points of the flight such as your route, and its main navigational features, as well as the restricted or prohibited airspace which could affect the flight, landing requirements of the destination, weather, and instruction as to what to do should an out-landing be necessary. Do not depart on your first cross-country flight without such a briefing.

Once you have planned and been briefed, your way is clear to getting airborne on what will almost certainly be one of the most memorable flights of your life. But before getting into the cockpit arrange your map and other items so that you can readily get at them without distracting yourself from flying. I wonder how many pilots have taken off with their maps out of reach, even sitting on them. . . .

Once airborne it will be worthwhile if you local soar for perhaps half an hour before you set course away from the airfield. This will enable you to settle down mentally and to adjust your flying to the prevailing conditions, and it will also give you an opportunity to look down your projected track and to note both the initial navigational features on the route and the prevailing weather conditions. I believe this is an important element in successful cross-country flying as it helps to ensure that the first few miles of the flight pass without incident; you know the route to take and you know what soaring conditions to expect.

As we discussed earlier, the height to which you should climb before setting course is not fixed. Certainly there is merit in setting an absolute lower limit of, say, 3000 feet (1000 metres) to allow for sufficient height to complete a successful out-landing, but, as we have already seen, you must take account of the depth of the convective layer as well. As a general rule, therefore, I suggest you aim to climb to near the top of the workable convective layer, or to near cloudbase, before you set heading.

Once you are on your way you must make a conscious effort to divide your time sensibly between soaring and navigation. Obviously, staying airborne until you reach your goal must be your prime concern, but, equally, it is important to make sure that you actually arrive at the correct goal and not at any place that just happens to be more than thirty miles (fifty kilometres) away from base. In many areas of the world airspace restrictions are such that the future of gliding there depends on pilots adhering to the regulations and keeping out of certain areas. A pilot ballooning down-wind on his first cross-country flight without a care for basic navigation is just the individual who can threaten our freedom to fly.

I am reluctant to say how much time you should devote to navigaton on your first cross-country flight because it is influenced by so many variables. However, as a very rough guide, a figure of up to ten per cent of your total time en route may well be required. Certainly you should not be spending half your time on navigation. If, indeed, you find this to be the case it implies that you have spent insufficient time during your local soaring exercises on this aspect of flying. (Obviously there will be periods on any flight when navigation demands extraordinary attention, but I am considering the overall flight.) Having noted the main navigational features of the first few miles whilst you were settling down in my suggested initial thirty minute period of local soaring, the first part of your cross-country should be straightforward from a navigation point of view. This will leave you, therefore with plenty of time to devote to soaring.

The first consideration is to select a route in the air which maximises the opportunity for flying through obvious areas of lift. To do this you may have to deviate from your straight line navigational route but it will make the task of finding thermals much easier. I am thinking particularly of soaring weather offering cumulus, when it will be possible, quite frequently, to find a route taking you under several clouds. Figure 11 illustrates this point. However, in deviating from track you will be flying a route displaced from the line on your map and, therefore, this will place a premium on your having done your navigational pre-study

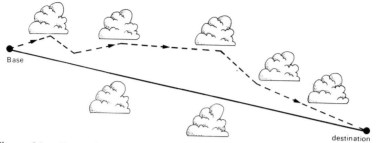

Figure 11.   Typical deviation from track

thoroughly if you are to minimise the risk of becoming lost. This is why I have said that it is important to study the first few miles of your route from the vantage point you get whilst local soaring; it will enable you to orientate readily your proposed route from a soaring viewpoint in relation to the track needed to reach the goal. It literally gives you a chance to 'get your bearings'.

It is normal for first cross-country flights to be undertaken in weather where cumulus clouds will be indicators of thermals, and there is little that needs adding to what I have already said about techniques for locating the lift under these conditions. However, in the excitement of your first real trip away from base it will be easy to allow your concentration to relax for all sorts of reasons and you could, for example, miss the subtle changes in the clouds which may mark their decay with the result that you soon find yourself looking for a landing area. The moral is clear; practise as many aspects of cross-country flying as possible before you put all the elements of the exercise together on your first cross-country flight, and ensure that you concentrate fully when you finally cut loose and fly away from the security of home.

Blue thermal cross-country flying presents somewhat different problems, the obvious and most significant one being the location of thermals, and for this reason initial cross-country flights are not normally conducted under such conditions, but, of course, there may well be exceptions. However, whilst the techniques for such location have been discussed in the chapter on local soaring, I can add a few useful points here. You may find it worthwhile to consider the problem further in case you find yourself encountering blue conditions on even part of your initial cross-country flight.

Ideally the most useful thing you can do is to try and establish the pattern of the blue thermals before you leave the airfield. The areas you should concentrate on are threefold. First, it will be useful to establish whether the thermals are forming into streets and, if so, what their alignment is in relation to the track of your intended flight. Second, I suggest you determine the general structure of the thermals, particularly as regards whether they are long-lived or of only short duration. If they are short-lived you will need to determine the depth of the thermal; it often happens that the thermal bubble is only a few hundred feet deep, so that a glider joining it below another glider which is climbing well can experience no lift at all, only the characteristic turbulence which marks the tail-end of a thermal. However, as we have already discussed, with such short-lived thermals one normally finds that fresh bubbles come off the same general source and form upwind of the decaying one. So, the aim of your local soaring before starting off cross-country should be to find out the general pattern of thermal formation so that you know what to expect en route and also how to handle the situation. Finally, you will find it useful to establish the frequency of thermals and the distance between successive ones. If they seem wide apart then you must remember to climb near the top of each good one if you are to stand a reasonable chance of finding the next one at a comfortable height above the ground.

Whether the thermals are marked by cloud or are blue you must remember that the main aim of your first cross-country is to complete it as planned. You should attempt to play the flight cautiously so that if possible you stay above the height at which a field landing becomes a consideration. Over good terrain this means staying higher than about 2000 feet (600 metres) above ground level. If you are to do this then it may well mean that you will need to pay only limited attention to speed flying and rather more attention to staying aloft. I suggest therefore that you set the speed ring for a nominal climb of, say, one knot and fly the relatively low speeds thus demanded. This will give you a reasonable compromise between average speed and survival. There is actually a clear mathematical relationship between the two which says, in essence, that under any given soaring conditions the faster your cruising speed between thermals the greater the probability of your not locating another thermal before you meet the ground. First cross-countries are not the time for emulating the pundits; fly cautiously and stay high.

Throughout the flight you must remember that safety is your main concern and you will need to bear in mind the possibility of having to make an out-landing. It should be unlikely if you are flying on a day with reasonable weather and if you have followed the general suggestions I have outlined, but there is always an element of luck! So, if you find yourself descending below about 2000 feet (600 metres) above ground level you should increase your attention to the terrain below, so as to locate suitable landing areas. Also, increase the emphasis you place on navigation because should you land out, it is advantageous to know where you are. (Try to avoid the need for the 'where have I landed?' question, unless you wish to embarrass yourself!)

As you descend you must progressively shift your attention from soaring to the task of selecting a landing area, until, by the time you are at circuit height your complete attention should be devoted to the task of flying the pattern and the landing. What you must avoid is the temptation to try and work a thermal encountered at low height whilst you are in the pattern for landing. This is the surest way to an accident and is something that even the most experienced cross-country glider pilots only attempt with caution.

The height of the ground will vary from place to place but determining your height above ground level need not be as daunting as it appears at first sight. The first thing you can do to help yourself is to set your altimeter to read your base airfield's height above sea-level; this will then enable you to subtract the height of the ground over which you are flying from that indicated on the altimeter in order to arrive at your actual height above the ground. This method assumes, of course, that you have a good idea where you are and also that you know how to read heights of the ground from the map.

In setting your altimeter to read heights above sea-level you are assuming that the atmospheric pressure will be the same over the whole area in which you plan to fly. In reality this is seldom the case, and you must therefore expect errors of a few hundred feet when landing some distance away from your base. Likewise, since pressure patterns in the atmosphere change with time you must expect similar errors at the end of a long flight even when landing back at your base. This problem can be overcome by using the forecast area pressure setting for the time and area in which you plan to operate; this is basically what power pilots do when flying cross-country at lower altitudes. The difficulty for glider pilots is the obvious one of obtaining the pressure setting in the first place, not having ready access to the air traffic control service which normally provides this information, and even having obtained it there is no guarantee that setting it on the altimeter sub-scale will produce the right altimeter reading. Alas, from my observation the calibration of the altimeter sub-scale with reference to the height needles is not always carried out on gliders, although it ought really to be.

The final aspect of your first cross-country to consider is the arrival at your destination. This particular flight of yours is no time to carry out a finely judged final glide. Instead, you should continue soaring flight at about the cruising height appropriate for the day until you are in sight of, and in comfortable gliding range of, the destination. Moreover, you must not descend until you have clearly identified your destination and at the same time established from observation the landing direction and area in use, together with other pertinent information. Don't allow your concentration to lapse during the approach and landing; you may well feel elated at having reached your goal but the trip is not over until the glider is safely parked.

If it all works out well your first cross-country flight will give you the distance qualification for your Silver Badge, but, life being what it is, you may find that you fail to make the requisite distance on your first attempt and you have to try again. Don't be downhearted – learn from your mistakes and take the attitude that you gained much useful experience from your first attempt. With gliding the attitude to take to misfortune is not 'if only I had done so', but 'now what can I learn from that experience so that I can prevent it happening again.' On that optimistic note we will now look at the philosophy and practice of more advanced cross-country flying.

6
Advanced cross-country flying

I am convinced that the most effective way to learn is to limit the learning process to relatively short, concentrated bursts of time, and then, immediately after such periods, make a conscious effort to assess progress. In gliding terms this implies that the shorter cross-country flights are better for learning the basic skills than the longer ones. On long flights, of say five hours or so, you obtain a kaleidescope of experiences, so many in fact that it is hard to draw specific lessons from amongst the mass of minor errors you probably made on the flight. On a shorter flight, of say two hours, the problem is simpler; lessons are more easily drawn, noted and remembered, and I think this is the best way to train. For medium performance gliders, I therefore recommend the 100 kilometre triangle as a very good exercise to begin with. Obviously, with a higher performance machine, or under very good gliding conditions, this distance is too short and a 150 kilometre or 200 kilometre triangle would be more appropriate.

The four main areas of practice you should concentrate on during these flights are: start line procedures and techniques, routine soaring over varying terrain and under a variety of convective conditions, turning point techniques and, the final glide back to base.

'Racing' starts

Achieving a satisfactory 'racing' start to a flight is a little bit more difficult than it might seem at first glance but, equally, it can make a substantial contribution to the overall success of the flight especially when you are seeking to achieve the maximum average speed. To recap and expand on what we discussed in Chapter 4. There are three main factors to consider when preparing to cross the start line: first you must take account of the height at which you cross; second, the speed; and third, and probably the most important, the soaring conditions along the first few miles of your track. There will also be a number of purely tactical factors to bear in mind when you progress to competition flying, such as the position of certain other competitors, particularly those who are lying close to you in the cumulative scores; you may wish to start just after them and then use them as pace setters. Alternatively, it can also pay to lead the field yourself. However, for now, we'll content ourselves with the mechanics of flying rather than the tactics, and leave that for later.

Looking to the details, an ideal start is one in which you cross the line at maximum permitted height, normally 3281 feet (1000 metres) above ground level, as laid down by the International Sporting Code, at maximum kinetic energy (maximum permitted indicated airspeed and maximum permitted all up weight), and is one which takes you into a strong thermal up to the operating height for the day within the first mile or two after crossing the line. If you succeed in bringing all these features together in the one start you will have done very well indeed and you need read this section no more, unless you feel that your good start was luck. Alas, things seldom work out that neatly, and normally you will have to accept compromises. It will, therefore, be useful if, in the next few paragraphs, we examine each of these three features in some detail.

If you cross the starting line above 1000 metres your start will be invalidated and for competition or record purposes the subsequent flight will be null and void. Height verification for competitions is normally by ground-based height finder but for record flights it is by inspection of the barograph by the Official Observer after the flight.

To cross the line at maximum kinetic energy you should aim to combine both maximum height, maximum speed and maximum all up weight into the one event. Bearing in mind the points mentioned in Chapter 4, you will have to ascertain the order of height loss needed by the particular glider you are flying in order to accelerate to the desired starting speed. However, you may find it useful to note that the point at which to start the dive can normally be judged by the apparent angle between you and the start line, with reference back to your height. This is something else you can really only learn from experience, so you must be prepared for trial and error. However, in determining when to begin the acceleration, and, also, how steep to make the dive, you must take account of the convective conditions you are likely to encounter on the way to the line itself. If you pass through thermals you may find you arrive high over the line and the converse is obviously true as well. To minimise these problems, I think you will find it useful to accelerate initially to about 80 knots (150 kph) and cruise at that speed towards the start line, and then, depending on the height remaining as you approach the line, you can accelerate up to the placard maximum speed, or a lower safe speed if there is heavy turbulence; you then sustain this speed until you have passed over the line. Once you have crossed you can convert the speed to height and slow down to the most favourable cruising speed for the prevailing weather conditions. However if, as you run-in for the start, you hit strong thermals and look like being high at the line you can then steepen your glide by increasing your speed, to something approaching maximum safe speed for the prevailing conditions, somewhat earlier than you originally intended. Conversely, if you encounter sink you will need to conserve your height and only increase your speed to the maximum at the last moment. In some cases you may need to return to a thermal and top-up with height for a fresh start. I must stress, however, that it is *vital* to observe the placarded speed limits for the glider and you should realise that aircraft design criteria allow very little margin for error as regards excess speed.

It is worth mentioning that some competition organisers lay down a specific speed for all gliders to use for the start-line crossing. For the pilot this poses no real problems and, in fact, it can make the whole procedure much simpler.

To achieve maximum kinetic energy you need the glider to be as heavy as possible, consistent with the flight placards. This raises the question of how much water ballast to carry and you may need to carry a maximum load, more than would normally be the case in the prevailing thermal conditions, purely to allow a greater potential for height gain during the zoom after the line crossing. Providing that you find you can climb high enough prior to the start to achieve sufficient height and speed at the line crossing, I can see no real objection to taking off with a heavy load of ballast as a matter of routine. I therefore suggest that you consider the idea of taking off with full or nearly full ballast, retaining it for the start and then only dumping sufficient thereafter to ensure that you achieve an adequate rate of climb in relation to other gliders. Obviously, this will not be without its problems; in particular, you will need to be very careful not to dump water on other gliders because this is regarded as extraordinarily unsporting and not without danger (it increases the stalling speed for the glider being rained upon). You will also need to ensure that your glider's water jettison system is in good working order and that the valves re-seat fully; you will also need to know exactly how much water is released in any given time.

If this all sounds like too much trouble then do not worry as you will not lose out to any great extent if you content yourself before flight with merely ballasting for the anticipated conditions; I am only pointing out all possible advantages.

The pull-up after the line crossing should be gentle, say, not more than 1.3 g, as any firmer pull will create excessive lift dependant drag which will merely negate your potential height gain from speed. Likewise, make sure that you do not initiate the pull-up until you have actually passed over the line; doing so prematurely may put you above the start line height measuring frame at the critical moment. If it is practical, you may find it worthwhile waiting until you hear the start line observer say 'line' over the radio, which will normally be at the instant of your line crossing, before you convert surplus speed to height.

Finally, at all times keep up a thorough and continuous lookout for other gliders, especially those which may have slipped underneath you and those which could be above you as you zoom. The start gate and start line is a congested place.

The last ingredient for a good start is the necessity to contact a good strong thermal soon after the start line crossing; what you must avoid is using a mediocre thermal for your initial climb after the start line crossing as this will tend to set the standard for the rest of the flight, as we discussed earlier in Chapter 4. To help you achieve this, devote some of your attention whilst local soaring prior to the start to establishing the pattern of thermal strength and distribution, and then to setting yourself a 'target' thermal strength which you should aim to locate and use throughout the remainder of the flight. You will also find it worthwhile finding out the height band in which the thermals are strongest so that during the rest of the flight you can try to keep within this band. In considering the start itself, you will find it best to plan your start line crossing and your glide to the first thermal thereafter so that you do not descend below this height band. To help you locate this first and most important thermal you can use the familiar indications given by clouds, or follow other gliders which appear to be climbing well. If you have a bit of the gambler instinct in you, you may wish to content yourself with heading out on track in the hope of finding a suitable thermal at random, particularly if conditions are blue. This last course of action sounds rather *ad hoc* but is a sound method so long as you are prepared to return for a fresh start if you fail to locate your thermal by the requisite height. However, be warned, it takes self-discipline to do this because once you have started out on course the desire to get on with the flight is strong and the mental effort required to counter this and to return to the start line is appreciable. With that being my final thought on 'racing' starts let us now turn to the routine of cross-country soaring.

Cross-country soaring

I believe the most important points to remember whilst on cross-country flights are: first, the need to plan well ahead, with the objective of leaving yourself several options for lift, and second, the need to pay as much attention as possible to decision making. To my mind, everything else is subordinate to these two points.

Planning well ahead may sound a simplistic and obvious notion but, as I know from my own experience, I have often caught myself out flying down a route without any really clear idea as to the best way ahead. (I am sure other pilots must have had the same experience.) When there is cumulus to mark both thermal development and their distribution the problem is, in fact, almost as difficult as when thermals are blue. The reason is that it takes much practice and observation to be able to read cloud development with such precision that by the time you actually get to a specific cloud the lift distribution below it is as you anticipated. It is quite easy to plan an 'instantaneous' cross-country under cumulus conditions by just looking at the sky and saying to yourself 'I would go from there to there to there, etc.' Doing it is quite another matter.

The key, to my mind, lies in developing the ability to 'read' clouds as indicators of lift and also in learning to appreciate the various stages of their development. Likewise, you must learn to recognise the various phases of convection so that you can observe the sky and assess the areas which are likely to be under strong convection by the time you would reach them in a glider. To illustrate how important this skill can be, you only have to consider the common occurrence of two gliders flying down a similar route and separated by, say, ten minutes. One of the pilots can have a first class, quick and easy passage, but the other may find himself having to use decaying thermals and poor lift generally. The second glider traversed the area in the wrong stage of its 'cycling' when thermals were in their dissipation phase. What the second pilot should have done was to examine the sky ahead and, if it had seemed to be good and convective whilst he was still a fair distance away, say fifteen to twenty miles (thirty kilometres), he should have expected the good area in question to be in decay by the time he reached it. He should, therefore, have been prepared to move his planned route to one side – normally upwind – to an area which, at the moment he examined it, appeared to be fairly blue with only small cumulus. As a very general rule this works quite well, but, as always in soaring, there can be no hard and fast rules for success. There is no substitute for detailed observation of the sky as a matter of habit over a long period as by this you will gain experience of the air's behaviour and you will be able to gauge the probable degree of lift in various conditions.

Planning ahead under blue thermal conditions is to some extent easier because much of it can be done on the ground before take-off. Under blue conditions the lack of cloud cover ensures that all areas of countryside are heated uniformally and so thermal distribution will be reasonably predictable.

Areas of ground which absorb most heat will be the areas which spawn the most frequent thermals, and this should be borne in mind when planning a cross-country flight in blue conditions. I would always consider using areas where differential heating is likely, such as built-up areas, open country adjacent to forests, sun-facing slopes of hills, and indeed hilly areas generally. There are, of course, many other sources of thermals; over hot desert or scrub, the best thermals often come off the darker areas, although this is not always so.

The nature of both the surface soil and the sub-soil, together with the water content of the ground, has a direct bearing on the strength and the frequency of thermals produced. In very general terms, as there are always exceptions, ground which is well drained will offer better thermals than damp regions. Limestone and chalk soils are normally better than clay for this reason, although well drained clay can be quite good as well. Sand is more difficult to generalise about and does not seem to follow any set rules. In England, for example, sandy soils are very good for producing thermals, but in parts of Texas, as I nearly found to my cost once, this does not always apply. So find out about the type of ground below you before you fly over it and also check with pilots who know the area well where the best regions for thermals are.

The technique I use on a flight under blue thermal conditions is essentially one of attempting to find the strong thermals, which are necessary if one is to achieve a high average speed, by arranging my flight to pass over, or just downwind of, likely sources. This does not mean that worthwhile thermals will not be found at random elsewhere but it is merely a practical way of maximising your chances of finding them. In blue conditions you are not likely to find the best thermals unless you deliberately plan your route to pass through an area where they will probably be, and you may find it worthwhile to highlight possible thermal sources on your map before flight. However, if blue convection is deep, say 5000 feet (1500 metres) or more, then it is perfectly reasonable to fly down track and rely on pure chance to find suitable thermals for you. The snag with shallow blue convection, as we discussed in Chapter 1, is that there is insufficient time or distance coverage between the top of the convective layer and the height needed for making a successful out-landing pattern, to afford a reasonable opportunity for thermal contact. It is in this situation that glider pilots tend to fly in groups ('gaggle' being the jargon) as, by so doing, a larger area can be swept in the search for thermals. This potential advantage from gaggle flying is totally negated if all pilots play 'follow the leader' and fly in a vague line-astern formation. There is also a further disadvantage when they all try to thermal together, in that no one glider obtains the optimum climb available, because each pilot will need to manoeuvre so as to maintain safe separation from others rather than to take full advantage of the thermal. It also has the drawback that such gaggles often seem to find and stay with the weaker thermals. (It may just be that the thermal has died in the lower levels by the time I always slide in underneath!)

The surest sign of a strong blue thermal is a glider turning steeply; if you see one and can join him at a similar height then you should be in for a worthwhile climb. If you join him well below you may find only the remnants of the thermal. On balance, therefore, there is much to be said for operating on your own under blue conditions but you must be prepared to work down to a lower height than you would normally accept. This will inevitably involve a greater risk of an out-landing but, equally, you will probably achieve a faster rate of climb than if you operated in a gaggle, and so gain a greater average speed. It is up to you to weigh up the options and the risks and to choose for yourself.

If there is any significant wind it will pay you to pre-plan the emergency use of any suitable hills or ridges on or adjacent to your track. Whether the day offers cumulus or blue thermals, a ridge is invariably an excellent trigger for thermals and, if all else fails but the wind blows, you can resort to hill soaring. Whilst you are airborne you are still in a position to complete the flight. Once on the ground . . . .

There are, of course, many other elements of the flight you can pre-plan but I believe the foregoing considerations are the most important. But when you have considered all these points you will gain much by just sitting down with the map and visualising the flight. It will also be useful to study the sky as much as possible whilst you are waiting for take-off. If there is cumulus then try to establish its pattern of development and decay, and take note as well of the wind speed at flying height, as indicated by the movement of cumulus. Also, as we discussed in Chapter 1, try to observe whether the cumulus has a rolling motion or a straight-forward bubble type formation. If it rolls, this indicates a marked wind effect on the thermal with the lift being upwind of the cloud; if there is a bubble formation, there will probably be easy soaring immediately below the cloud. However, remember that, in general, thermals will be short-lived early in the day. Whilst waiting on the ground take note, also, of gliders which are soaring already: note their height, their apparent rate of climb and whether they are turning tightly or just meandering. All these pointers can help you to anticipate the likely soaring conditions and enable you to settle down quickly once airborne.

You will need to continue planning ahead throughout the flight if you are to achieve your best performance. I have found that it pays handsome dividends to think well beyond the next thermal and to keep updating your tactical plan; you could say you should think ten miles (twenty kilometres) ahead, but under good conditions of deep convection this figure would be unrealistically low. Obviously, there will be many situations in which it will be impossible to think or plan this far ahead but, as long as you are aware of the principle, you will have helped yourself enormously.

The next main point to consider is the need to try to leave yourself several options for lift whenever practical. Basically all this entails is making a deliberate attempt to ensure that you do not commit yourself to just one cloud or lift source without leaving sufficient height to reach another, should your first fail to work satisfactorily. As I have said, this should be your *objective* rather than your firm resolve, as it will not always be possible to do this. Having several options for lift will also reduce the risk of an out-landing which is always there when working the flight down to low altitude. Indeed, when you are low, you virtually have no options and you have to accept any lift which turns up, regardless of its strength.

Your first intended lift source should, as far as possible, be sufficiently high that, should it fail to produce anything, an out-landing would remain only a very remote possibility. If your second source didn't work either then your height should still be such that you now only need take a more cautious approach to the flight in order to avoid getting too low. Only if your third source fails should survival become the main concern. This approach is very simplified and will rarely be true in any specific instance, but it should at least give you an idea of what to aim for.

When you have gained more experience, you won't need to fly with several lift sources in mind, largely because your ability to anticipate lift correctly will have improved and you will be better able to rely on your initial judgement, particularly when the soaring weather is straightforward. However, when the weather conditions are at all difficult I feel that it will always be worthwhile reverting to the principle of keeping several options for lift open. I certainly use it under such situations and, also, I try to keep it at the forefront of my mind even under good conditions because I feel more confident about discarding my first choice; I know that I have a second readily at hand.

With modern cross-country and competitive gliding placing such a premium on fast average speeds, there is a strong tendency to press on at all costs regardless of the prospects for lift ahead; in these circumstances a premature out-landing can easily result. Remember that, whilst you are still airborne there is still a chance of success and you must therefore continually assess conditions ahead. If the situation is one in which you are unlikely to be successful then you must make the disciplined and difficult decision either to divert around the difficult area or to obtain sufficient height to cross it, or, in extreme circumstances, to hold your position in the soarable weather until the conditions ahead improve sufficiently to let you through. There is no point in rushing on ahead like a blinkered racehorse if to do so merely precipitates an out-landing.

I myself find it particularly difficult to play the waiting game at the edge of a bad patch of weather; it seems so out of place in racing gliding. However, in reality the time involved is often minimal, seldom more than a few minutes, and is usefully taken up with working out a route around the bad patch or in gaining sufficient height to glide across it. There will be exceptional occasions when you will have to wait for extended periods for a route ahead to open up. But you must be satisfied that the weather will not deteriorate while you wait.

In crossing an area of poor weather the glide angle calculator can be very useful. From the cockpit the prospects for getting across a gap will often appear daunting but whilst, say, fifteen miles (thirty kilometres) may seem a very long way, it need actually take no more than 3000 feet (1000 metres) to traverse. Indeed, in a good Open Class machine 2000 feet (600 metres) is probably nearer the mark. The advantage of using the calculator is that you can quantify the height required and set off across difficult areas with some confidence. Assuming no undue sink is encountered, and that you allow sufficient height for the glide, you should be able to reach the other side with enough height to conduct a short search for lift. Moreover, during the long glide across the area you will have more than enough time to maintain a watch on conditions ahead so that you can adjust your heading to take you to the most promising lift source. It will be quite common to find that the extra attention you will have paid to studying the likely thermal conditions ahead result in you finding excellent lift at the first attempt. This substantiates my third point – concentration brings worthwhile results.

The ability to concentrate on the immediate problem is probably the single biggest factor separating the brilliant pilot from the ordinary. In simple terms, if you find you have time to think of things other than the immediate job of soaring then you are not devoting your full attention to the flight. This is not to say that you should not sit back from time to time and admire the view and generally relax but when you do so you must be aware that it will detract from your potential performance.

I suggest you make a conscious effort to ensure that no more than about three minutes elapse between each major decision (those where you decide which route to follow, when to circle in any thermal which may be found, when to leave the thermal, when to slow down in lift, and when to speed up in sink). You must go all out to break the natural tendency to just sit back and let things happen, and, instead, you must be firm with yourself and take full charge of events.

Another way to improve your flying and to develop your concentration is to simulate decision making whilst still on the ground. In my experience, this is a remarkably effective method and really produces good results. All that you need to do is to sit down and relax, or just lie in bed if you feel that is more appropriate, and then visualise various situations in the air, imagining what you believe to be the right course of action. It sounds easy, and it is. Also, to some extent your self confidence can be improved in this way – providing you arrange for your imaginary decisions to turn out successfully! However, to be realistic it is best to arrange for some to go wrong, so that you can then give yourself the chance to correct them.

Glider handling techniques

Turning now to the flying itself, the precise handling techniques used when flying in thermals deserve close attention because the essence of fast cross-country gliding is to spend as little time as possible climbing and the maximum amount of time cruising. By using the right handling techniques the rate of climb can be usefully increased, thus directly contributing to your achieved speed. In this respect there are two areas for consideration: the techniques which can be used in a conventional climb–cruise–climb cross-country flight, and those which are appropriate for 'dolphin' style gliding.

In considering conventional thermalling flight, the points to pay special attention to can be considered under three headings: the entry to the thermal, the climb itself, and the exit.

A good thermal entry is one in which you decelerate from cruising speed progressively as you fly into the rising air and in which you then establish a turn which is accurately centred on the lift and requires little further adjustment after the first complete turn. To achieve this takes a high level of concentration and discipline – concentration to work out the likely pattern of the thermal and its characteristics from the cloud indications and from the turbulence pattern you experience around and on the edge of the thermal, and discipline to ensure that you act on your deductions. For example, it is easy to encounter a thermal-like turbulence and to begin slowing down, as if by habit, well before you are positive that it offers worthwhile lift. But if, in fact, the turbulence turns out to be of no significance then you will have gained nothing by slowing down; on the contrary you will have lost out because of the inherent losses incurred in conversion of speed to height, and vice-versa. Likewise, you may have a propensity to turn in one direction but you must not let this override your assessment of the correct way to turn on entry into the thermal. Don't forget that you cannot afford such errors in competitive flight, as they all lose you precious seconds.

During the climb you will gain most by establishing the glider in a steady turn with the correct pitch attitude for the required speed. Do not 'chase' the speed but, with the attitude constant, allow the speed to fluctuate around the figure you want. Avoid undue use of the controls as this creates unnecessary drag; instead be content to let the glider's own stability do much of the flying for you and only use the controls to correct major deviations from the desired flight path. Obviously, some types of glider lend themselves more to this approach than others but the main thing is to avoid thrashing the controls all around the cockpit as you fly. Just how often have you followed another pilot in a thermal and seen the rudder of his machine being moved continually? (Similar to propelling a small dinghy, but it doesn't work in the air.) Just let *him* keep on doing it because if you heed my advice and keep all the controls, especially the ailerons, as steady as possible you will outclimb him easily.

A word of caution concerning thermal entries made from cruising speed. The action of slowing down converts speed to height and the height gain in the resultant zoom climb can be anything from a few feet to several hundred. You should, therefore, take special care to check whether there are any other gliders in the thermal you enter and, if so, you must keep your eye on them throughout the manoeuvre. Don't forget that inertia has its part to play in the proceedings and once your machine has established any substantial speed in any direction (such as the velocity you may have in relation to another glider before a collision) it takes a finite time and distance to correct the situation. In other words, anticipation is all important. Remember that if you and another glider are flying on converging courses then you will collide if you maintain a constant relative angle to each other. The secret is to achieve a changing relative angle.

I will not discuss the various techniques for finding and staying in the core of a thermal as this is adequately discussed in a number of other books which deal with the fundamentals of gliding.

Leaving the thermal efficiently can give you a useful advantage over a pilot who merely meanders his way out and then sets heading. The first point to bear in mind is that thermals reduce in strength as they approach their ceiling. You must therefore discipline yourself to leave before the climb rate deteriorates too much, bearing in mind your height above ground and the distance to the next thermal, and I stress again that the two-thirds rule is a good one to use if in doubt. Once you have made your decision to leave, you will find it worthwhile to begin your acceleration to cruising speed before you hit the surrounding sinking air. One particularly useful technique is to accelerate during your final circle in the thermal; this can have the added advantage of disguising the acceleration from a fellow competing pilot flying in the same thermal and can give you a few useful seconds over him. The pilot who wins is the one who saves the most seconds!

'Dolphin' style gliding is basically very straight-forward and easy to learn and is, in fact, only a modification of conventional thermalling technique. The techniques work best with very high performance machines but they can be used, though less effectively, in lower performance gliders.

The first, most fundamental principle to try and satisfy is to achieve a route through the air which follows the areas of maximum energy. If you can fly for prolonged periods with wings level then, even if you detour 30° or so off track to enable you to do so, you will probably still achieve a higher average speed than if you had flown in the conventional climb/cruise mode for that sector of the flight. The higher the performance of the glider you are flying then the more pronounced this becomes. This is because the flat glide angle of high performance machines means that the relatively small height loss in each glide can often be regained in full during a slow speed flight through the next thermal. Having chosen a path of maximum atmospheric energy, the technique is basically one of following the guidance given by the speed-to-fly ring; fly fast in sink and slow down in lift. If the lift is strong you can afford to bring the speed back to the lowest practical figure and to carry out 'S' turns in order to prolong the time spent in lift. Indeed, it is this zooming and meandering flight which is characteristic of 'Dolphin' flying. Basically, the higher performance machines will be capable of achieving cross-country flight in this style with relative ease, given the right conditions, whereas the lower performance types will gradually lose height overall and will need to resort to conventional circling climbs more frequently.

I must emphasise that in 'Dolphin' style flight one of the important things to do is to seek out and use areas where lift is aligned in the general direction of your flight. Perhaps it will be worthwhile just to remind ourselves of some of the more common types. There is the 'classic' cloud street, which was discussed in Chapter 1, there is also the convergence or shearline street, such as a sea breeze front, and there is the wave influenced street. Both of the two latter types will normally have their clouds aligned cross-wind. One of the secrets of successful high speed cross-country flying is to make a real effort to search out and use such lines of lift as much as possible. As I have said before, think nothing of making quite sizeable detours off track if so doing enables you to fly wings level for long periods. With practice you will find this technique remarkably effective and a most convincing way of improving your cross-country average speeds.

Flaps

Flaps on gliders can improve performance if they are used correctly. It is well worth noting that in general flapped aerofoils, when flown at the incorrect angle of attack perform much worse than unflapped ones, and accurate flying is therefore most important. Remember that flaps enable the pilot to vary the lift coefficient of the wing so that it is flown at the optimum angle of attack to the airflow for the prevailing speed and load factor.

In practice, the main point is that flap position is not entirely dependent upon speed, but, rather, on the lift demanded. Therefore, as you pull up into a thermal from high speed you should leave the flap in its negative setting, the reason being that at the high speeds from which a pull-up is initiated, you only need increase the angle of attack slightly to achieve the additional lift needed for the manoeuvre, and the wing can readily produce this without departing significantly from its optimum angle of attack. As the glider zooms, followed by a push-over the top of the zoom into a normal cruising attitude or into a thermal turn, very little lift is required, either because of the steep angle of the zoom or because of the reduced 'g' during the push-over. The flaps can therefore be left in their negative setting throughout these manoeuvres. You only need to put the flap down into the zero setting, or into the thermalling detent, when you actually want the full amount of lift required to support flight at the lower speed. Likewise on leaving the thermal, as soon as you ease the nose down you are demanding less lift from the wing so you can move to negative flap straight away; the action of raising the flaps will of itself change the speed because so doing reduces the drag of the wings and allows the glider to accelerate. In other words if, as you leave a thermal, you select flaps to negative and simultaneously hold the elevator steady, the glider will eventually accelerate to something near your desired cruising speed. However, this may take time and the process can be considerably speeded up by lowering the nose with elevator, in the normal manner.

In summary, flaps should not be regarded as anything other than an auxiliary control to enable the pilot to operate the wing efficiently throughout the speed range. They are straightforward to use and will become instinctive after only a few hours' practice.

Wind effect

As we have already seen, the wind has considerable influence on the way in which thermals behave and it also has a pronounced bearing upon the tactical conduct of the flight. There are two main points to bear in mind.

When flying cross-country with a strong crosswind, try to fly a little into wind of the track drawn on the map; this ensures that, should you have to use a weak thermal, you merely get drifted back on track in the process, rather than getting hopelessly downwind. Obviously, if thermal conditions are straightforward then there is no need to do this and, similarly, in high performance gliders wind is of less significance. The second point concerns flying into headwinds. Under these conditions every circle in a thermal drifts you back down track away from your turning point, so what you will need to do is to go all out to seek out cloud streets and other lines of lift to enable you to fly wings level as much as possible. It is also crucial that you consistently achieve the highest conceivable rate of climb under such conditions to make the most rapid progress possible into the wind. It is not time for bumbling!

Turning points

Average speeds can also be improved by developing a sound procedure for rounding turning points. Some of the basic photographic techniques were discussed in Chapter 4 but it will now be useful to discuss some of the tactical considerations.

The most common trick used to improve average speeds around turning points is to vary the height at which the point is rounded, depending upon whether it is upwind or downwind of the route being flown. If the leg being flown is into-wind then the turning point should be rounded at the lowest safe practical height and, if it is downwind, the converse applies. The logic behind this is straightforward; every time you stop to thermal you drift with the wind, and on an into-wind leg this means that you lose some of the ground you have already covered, which, in effect, gives you a reduction in cross-country speed. In extreme cases you may never reach the turning point at all!

Rounding an into-wind turning point at low altitude is merely an attempt to reduce, as far as is possible, the adverse effect of wind on the leg being flown. Another way of looking at it is to regard the low turning of the point as the use of your start line height to overcome the wind. For example, if you start the flight at maximum altitude and zoom after the line crossing you will have, say, 3500 feet (1100 metres) to play with. If you take a chance at the turning point and go round at 1000 feet (300 metres), you will, in effect, have been able to use 2500 feet (750 metres) of your initial height to help your penetration into the wind. Obviously by getting low there will always be the risk of an unscheduled out-landing but if you concentrate on the weather in the turning point region you will be able to anticipate likely thermals, and fly straight into them. This is what the expert and courageous do; I tend to turn somewhat higher which keeps the adrenalin flow down to manageable proportions!

Rounding a downwind turning point is a more leisurely affair as it generally pays to go round at or near the maximum height practical for the prevailing weather conditions. All the time spent circling on the leg running up to the turning point is beneficial as the wind will continue to drift you in your desired direction whilst you circle. However, this does not mean that a mediocre thermal on the leg running up to the turning point should be used if you have the opportunity to turn the point at low altitude and then glide to a strong thermal nearby. For example, if you are aware of vigorous lift beyond the turning point, caused by developing stubble fire or a series of dust devils, it would pay to glide out via the turning point, without stopping to sample thermals en route.

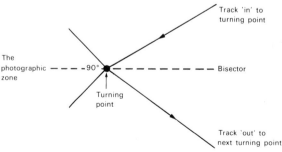

Figure 12.   Photographic zone

Whatever the circumstances, you will save precious seconds by turning as close as possible to the point. However, remember that the photographic zone centred on the point is at its smallest at the point itself, and while keeping as close to it as possible you must nevertheless be correctly positioned in the photographic zone; see Figure 12. Practice at the photographic techniques involved can best be obtained during local practice flights, as already discussed, and so all you should need to do on your cross-country flights is to run in to the turning point, dip the wing, 'click' the photographs – and continue to the next thermal. Anything more involved than this represents time wasted and a loss of potential speed.

Final glides

The techniques for final gliding vary considerably according to both weather conditions and the type of glider being flown. The simplest situation is one in which you anticipate no significant thermal activity after you leave your last thermal. In this case you need only climb to a height sufficient to reach your destination with a glide in at the speed dictated by the rate of climb achieved in the last thermal used, rather than by the anticipated climb in the next thermal. However, in practice you may find that you are unable to achieve sufficient height to warrant a glide at anything other than the speed for best glide angle, with perhaps a small margin of height if you are lucky, and in this situation there is little you can do in any tactical sense to improve your average speed. From a survival point of view it may pay you to make small detours over likely thermal sources in the hope of gaining sufficient extra height to make the glide less marginal, but you must weigh this up against the extra distance you will have to fly and the consequent extra height loss should you encounter no lift at all.

In normal circumstances you should be able to find a thermal for your final climb which gives you the same rate of climb as you experienced during the latter part of the flight; anything less than this should be discarded in the usual way unless it is clear that conditions ahead are poor and unlikely to give you anything better. However, it takes a measure of determination to do this as the temptation to get into your final glide as early as possible is very

Advanced cross-country flying

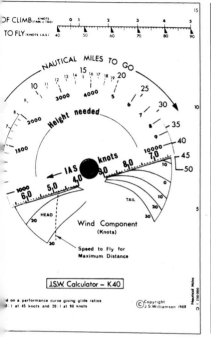

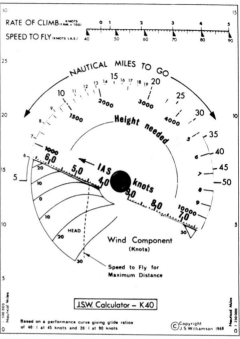

Left: final glide at speed for a 4 knot rate of climb = 80 knots
20 miles requires 5000 feet in zero wind
Right: final glide at speed for best gliding angle
20 miles requires 3000 feet in zero wind

strong and must be resisted if high average speeds are your
intention. Your aim should be to execute the final glide at the mean
cruising speed for the day. For planning the height required merely
set the calculator to the desired cruising speed against the expected
wind and read off the height needed against the distance to go. To
this you may wish to add a height margin, which will depend upon
the conditions anticipated. However, it is worth remembering
that a safety margin already exists in that extra gliding range can
be achieved by reducing speed on a final glide to a figure nearer
that for the best glide angle. The photos above show various
settings of a JSW calculator to illustrate these points.

From my experience, the above technique for establishing a final
glide is particularly suited to lower performance machines, whereas

for the high performance Open Class gliders a different system is more appropriate. These gliders are particularly well suited to 'Dolphin' type flying and can gain significantly from slowing down in any lift encountered, far more so than, say, the fifteen metre span machines. In an Open Class glider, therefore, I feel it is often better to begin the final glide as soon as you feel that you could just about reach the destination at best gliding angle. However, what you actually do in this situation is to fly at the cruising speed dictated by the last climb and rely upon lift encountered en route to make the glide possible at that speed. Any surplus height gained can be converted to speed during the glide. Obviously, if you anticipate no lift ahead then the glide should be undertaken at the calculated speed for the range, height and wind.

Ballast also affects the speed for the final glide, as indeed it does throughout the flight, and it should be taken into account, particularly for a marginal glide. In this situation it may be worth jettisoning some ballast in the last thermal to improve the climb, achieve a greater height in the thermal and so glide home more easily. On the other hand, keeping water on gives your glider its gliding angle at a higher speed than when it is lighter; this not only helps to increase your average speed but enables you to penetrate headwinds or areas of sink more readily, ensuring minimum height losses. Retaining ballast for the final glide is, therefore, normally advantageous.

The final glide bears heavily on the overall success of the flight; its importance is, of course, greater on short flights than on long ones. It is an area of gliding I have always found difficult, and I suspect I am not alone in this. In my case I invariably seem to have too much height and arrive over the finish line at maximum height and speed – but, then, I have on a few memorable but miserable occasions failed to make the finish line under perfectly soarable conditions purely by pressing on too hard and allowing insufficient height margin before setting out on the final glide. On balance, the cautious approach with spare height is probably the best bet but, although you may do well on average, you will probably not be the fastest round the course on individual days. The chap who presses on and takes a chance will be the fastest, but he will land short once in a while.

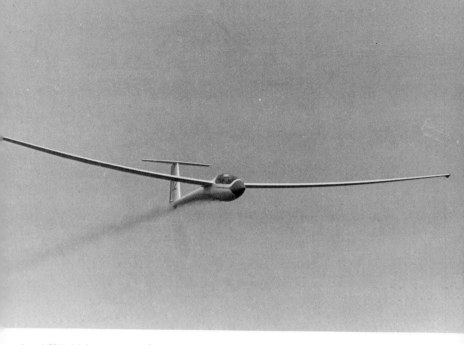

An ASW 20 jettisoning the water ballast and approaching the finish line (*Paul Bolton*)

Longer flights

When you feel that you have become reasonably adept at the shorter flights you should begin to extend yourself by working up to longer task flights of several hours. Certainly, before entering your first competition, you will need to be happy flying cross-country for trips lasting three hours as a minimum because only by doing so will you develop the necessary stamina for long competition flights. You will also gain much useful experience in coping with different soaring conditions; you will find you need to 'change gear' mentally when thermal strengths and cloud conditions vary. I have found this particular aspect of cross-country gliding very difficult as the rhythm of activity is broken and one has then to begin again and establish a fresh style of flying. However, this is all too common in competitive flying and it is obviously preferable to have some experience of it beforehand. Forewarned is forearmed.

Gliding Competitively

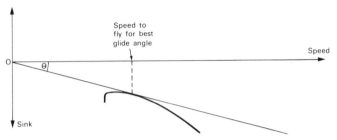

Figure 13.   Speed to fly for best glide angle

Speeds to fly

You may wonder why in this chapter I have not considered in any detail the techniques of so called 'speed flying' – the system of flying the speed indicated by both the thermal strength and the sink you experience on specific sections of the flight. I personally believe that a much greater contribution to achieved average speeds is made by correct tactical decision making in the air rather than by following theoretical speeds precisely. Much discussion in this chapter has been on tactics and I intend to emphasise the point by dwelling only briefly on the mechanics of speed flying.

The basic principle of cruising at a higher speed than that for circling flight has been known since the early days of soaring. However, Dr Paul MacCready of the United States is credited with developing the mathematics of the theory, and, particularly, with its application to the speed to fly devices we all take for granted today. The principle can most simply be explained by reference to the performance curve for the glider, commonly referred to as the 'polar curve', and all that needs to be appreciated is that the best ratio between the two axes, speed horizontally and speed vertically, is given by the tangent to the curve. This can be seen clearly from Figure 13.

Referring to Figure 13, a line drawn from the zero origin of both axes gives an angle, marked θ in this example, which is equal to the angle of descent. If you experiment in drawing other lines to the curve it will readily be apparent that the smallest angle occurs only when the line drawn is the tangent to the curve. No other

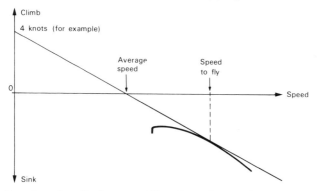

Figure 14.   Speed to fly for a specific achieved rate of climb

geometric construction does this. If the two axes are drawn to the same scale and are projected to a zero origin then A will be the 'best glide angle'. The speed to fly for the best glide angle is found by constructing a vertical line to the horizontal axis from the point of intersection of the tangent with the polar curve.

To determine the speeds to fly in a dynamic climb–cruise–climb situation the same principle is applied but modified slightly. Look at Figure 14; in a flight giving an achieved average climb rate of, say, four knots, a tangent to the polar drawn from the vertical axis at the four knot climb point gives the best speed for this situation. From this particular construction you can determine the *average speed* which could be achieved in a climb–cruise–climb flight using a specific thermal strength. This is given by the inter-section of the tangent with the horizontal axis, and, once again is only at a maximum when a tangent, as opposed to any other construction, is drawn. Again the speed to fly is given by the intersection of a vertical drawn from the tangent point to the horizontal axis.

The speed to fly in sinking air can be found in exactly the same way. When flying in sink you can consider the whole polar curve to be moved down the vertical axis by the amount of the sink. From this the speeds to fly in the sinking air for both best glide angle and for best average speed can be found by drawing a tangent, as before. However, to simplify the graphs, rather than moving the whole curve down the vertical axis the curve can be left alone and the sink applied from the up part of the vertical axis, as for lift. We must note, though, that we are dealing here in actual air mass sink, and the sink indicated on an ordinary 'raw' variometer would be the sum of both the air mass sink and that of the glider in still air for the speed being flown. This neglects any additional sink due to aerodynamic losses; rain, bugs, etc. Without going into further detail you will appreciate that the speed to fly, and thus the achieved overall cross-country speed, is related to the net result of the air mass up (lift) minus the air mass down (sink). This is a dynamic situation, changing throughout the flight.

The calibration of the speed to fly system of the variometer is found by reference to the polar curve for the glider and this is generally done by drawing a series of tangents for different rates of climb and sink and noting the relevant speeds to fly. These are then transferred to the speed to fly system. In flight, the only thing which matters is that we have the correct calibration for the variometer system we are using. One added refinement is to have calibrations for the glider both with and without water ballast; both can readily be displayed on one speed ring.

The variometer must be equipped with a really good total energy system, and, as I have said before, I firmly believe that this is far more important than any other aspect of instrumentation. With poor total energy you are likely to spend half your time chasing non-existent thermals, which is both inefficient and highly frustrating.

To remind you, for practical purposes in flight, the datum of the speed to fly system should be set to about half the indicated rate of climb, as this is approximately the average climb rate, and takes account of both the entry to and the exit from the thermal. Obviously, if the glider is equipped with an averager then the rate of climb can be determined with greater precision.

In cruising flight it is extremely tiring and indeed almost impossible to follow every speed change demanded by the speed to fly system and, in practice, it is easier to settle on a target cruising speed for the prevailing thermal strength and then only modify this speed if persistent sink or lift is encountered. This task can be made very much easier if the glider is equipped with a good speed director system; but anyway, even if your cruising speed is a little incorrect it will have only a very small effect on your average speed. Choose the best path through the air, follow the areas of lift, concentrate on the soaring and you will find that you produce consistently good results.

Wave flying

Finally, I believe I would be considered a kill-joy if I did not now talk briefly about wave flying with regard to cross-country and competition flying based on thermals.

Wave soaring is little practised in the course of such flying, largely, I believe, because the time taken to establish proper contact with the wave itself makes it difficult to achieve fast cross-country average speeds. Having said this, I should counter it by saying that under good wave conditions complete cross-country tasks, triangular and out and return, can be flown entirely in wave and at high average speeds. There still remains, however, the problem in contest and record flying of crossing the start line below the requisite 3281 feet (1000 metres) and then achieving a sufficiently rapid climb to give an overall satisfactory speed for the flight. The other factor to remember in wave based cross-country flying is the orientation of the wave system itself, which tends to dictate the type of task flown (Figure 15). To gain really high average speeds the task route should be aligned as nearly as possible with the axis of the wave because this will enable the flight to be made without the difficulties of crossing the wave system. There will, however, remain the problem of crossing the system on a triangular flight as one of the legs must inevitably be at a marked crossing angle to the main wave system. On such flights the point to bear in mind is the large height loss which can be experienced when crossing upwind from one wave to the next and, although 10,000 feet (3000 metres) may seem high, it can vanish in just a few minutes once you start moving around the wave system. Even over the relatively low mountains in Great Britain, where landing areas are good compared with those in other parts of the world, this situation becomes fraught with problems. Obviously, it is preferable to arrange the task so that your route takes you downwind from one wave to the next, rather than upwind. So before using wave in cross-country flights, you should either seek expert advice and briefing first or you should tackle it cautiously one step at a time.

There are occasions, during thermal based cross-country flights

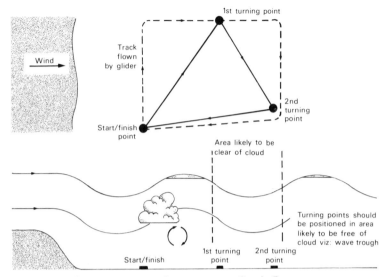

Figure 15.   The wave system dictates type of task flown

under wave conditions, when it will pay to work your way up into the wave itself, despite the time this may take. For instance, on cross-country flights when thermal activity is being dampened by the onset of a warm front, which is a good indicator of likely wave activity, I have known several cases in which pilots have worked wave induced thermals until they have contacted the wave proper and have then used the height so gained to complete the flight. A point to remember here is that extensive cloud cover frequently occurs under these conditions which will make subsequent navigation very difficult. It will also pose hazards for the descent if the safety altitude necessitated by neighbouring high ground and obstacles is not fully taken into account.

The merits of cross-country flying in wave rather than thermals can be put into perspective by the following account of two quite different approaches to a particular task which in the event, produced similar results.

In 1972 I was competing in the British National Championships at Shobdon, on the eastern edge of the main mass of the Welsh hills. The task was a short straight line race of 168 km from Shobdon to Dunstable and the weather forecast indicated a strong wind from the west which, in flight, would be a quartering tail

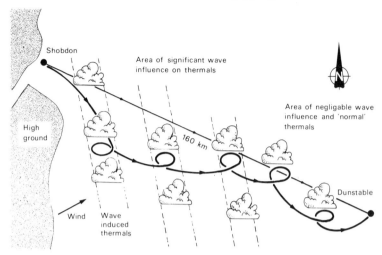

Figure 16.   168 km race from Shobdon to Dunstable

wind (see Figure 16). Difficult thermal conditions in the Shobdon area were predicted but they would improve towards Dunstable; significant wave influence over the western part of the route was forecast.

My own flight was relatively straightforward and involved the search for and use of thermals triggered by wave. On this occasion the waves were marked by medium level lenticulars and I could see scraggy looking cumulus clouds forming below the upgoing waves. I, therefore, worked my way up to the cloudbase in each area of cumulus before turning down track and picking up the tailwind component which whisked me rapidly to the next area of cumulus. So long as I remembered the wave induced nature of each thermal, and worked it accordingly, progress was quite straightforward, and I made the goal with the winning speed. However, close on my heels at the end of the day was Lemmie Tanner who had had quite a different flight – in fact he had had two flights! His first ended in a field not far from Shobdon, but, having been retrieved and re-launched (then allowed by contest regulations) he found that thermal activity was decaying fast under the influence of an advancing warm front. However, these conditions were ideal for good waves and he climbed above the partial overcast in wave to set

heading for Dunstable. After topping up in further waves en route he glided out to land at Dunstable with a speed very similar to mine. We had two separate approaches to the flight (albeit under somewhat different weather conditions) which produced very similar results. So – wave lift can sometimes have a part to play in cross-country and competition gliding, if you keep your eyes open and think flexibly.

In this chapter we have looked at some of the practical and philosophical factors you can usefully take into account in developing your flying towards the standard needed for competitive work. In the next chapter I will develop some of these points, with particular reference to the psychology of competitive success.

Opposite – flying a Nimbus 3 6000 ft in wave over Syerston

7

Competitions

Your first competition will probably teach you more about cross-country gliding than you have ever learnt before. It will be very enjoyable, but you should be prepared to find out that you are not as good a glider pilot as you had thought. You may be a 'natural' and do everything right but for most of us doing well in competition is something learned through trial and error. If you have carried out all the training we have discussed so far, your first competition flights should not prove too demanding – but you need to be prepared for a barrage of new experiences. It is all too easy to become demoralised when you find that the competition flights are not as straightforward as you anticipated.

Before competing you will find it very useful to have undertaken task flights from your base airfield, preferably on your own at first. Your measure of performance should be the time taken to complete the flight against your attempts at similar tasks. Naturally, you can include all the elements of a task, start and finish and turning point techniques, on such flights. However, the real character-building process starts when you begin to fly such tasks with other pilots, as only then will you begin to get a direct comparison of your performance with theirs. It can be a chastening experience but it is far better to have had it before the full scale competition; indeed, I think it is essential.

Preparation for a competition is all-important and can make the difference between both success and failure and between enjoyment and dissatisfaction. 'Preparation' not only means preparing the glider so that it is in the best possible condition but includes the whole range of equipment needed for the competition; maps, car, trailer and so on. But the most important piece of equipment is the pilot; an ill-prepared pilot is a poor candidate for success and, indeed, could even be said to be wasting his time and money by competing.

Preparing yourself for competition

The most important preparation for the pilot himself is psychological. We talked about this in the preceding chapter but it will be useful to consider the subject further here.

You need to cultivate a positive desire for achievement, as, to a large extent, you will achieve only the level of performance you anticipate for yourself. If you compete with the aim of just doing 'fairly well' then do not be surprised if you finish well down in the final results. As I suggested before, try visualising problems in flight, and how you would overcome them – this can be a very effective way to prepare yourself for competition.

Confidence is closely related to the desire for achievement but it is not always something which comes easily to people. Self-confidence is a definite attribute in competition gliding – over-confidence, however, is to be avoided as it leads to dangerous flying, whereas lack of confidence prevents the pilot from realising his full potential. To the over-confident pilot I can only say 'be careful', but it is the under-confident one who most needs help, and I will try to offer some here.

A glider pilot's self-confidence directly affects both his decision making in the air and the single-mindedness with which he executes those decisions. With low confidence comes caution, which can be a good thing if the weather is poor, but lack of confidence can cloud an otherwise rational decision and cause the pilot to be over-cautious. I have often found myself to be over-cautious (for instance, in taking excessive height or flying unnecessarily slowly) when I have known that an aggressive course of action would be best. Each time this has happened I have known very well that I was being over-cautious but I just did not seem to have the courage of my convictions. Analysing this I felt that my lack of determination was out of character; I had not been cautious during my routine practice cross-country flying and from this I concluded that I had allowed myself to become overawed by competition from other pilots. However, once I had acknowledged this fact, I found that I was most of the way towards overcoming the problem. Other pilots may find that their lack of confidence arises from other specific causes. For example, a pilot who has had only minimal cross-country flying experience will almost certainly find that this lack of experience will of itself lower his confidence level and cause unnecessary caution. But the main point to note is that over-caution leads to relatively low achieved cross-country speeds and it is, therefore, an area well worth concentrating on.

If you find that, despite practice, your confidence level is invariably low when you are under stress in competition, try looking at the problem dispassionately. Assuming that your practice flying outside competition has been successful, think about other occasions when you have felt unconfident, and how you have mastered the feeling successfully. Merely say to yourself 'I have successfully overcome a similar situation in practice and there is no logical reason why I should not be able to do the same in my present situation'. A positive thought process can be surprisingly beneficial; don't think of all the things that might go wrong, but consider that your actions *will* lead to success. Believe in yourself.

A positive desire for achievement is directly related to determination, although to my mind it is not exactly the same thing. You may enter a contest with a strong desire to excel but you then discover that as soon as things become difficult or you start to perform badly, your desire weakens and you merely content yourself with an average performance. This is where you must exert all your determination, override your defeatism and set your mind firmly on achieving the best possible results. Determination, therefore, can be seen as something which reinforces your intentions and sees you successfully through difficult periods in flight and in competition. It is a quality which you must make yourself aware of and one that you will need fully to cultivate if you are to surmount the many obstacles found in contest flying.

Determination, of course, varies between individuals and has a lot to do with influences and experiences affecting each person during upbringing and early adult life. It follows, therefore, that the level of determination in any individual may be increased providing the stimulus is strong enough. Obviously the younger you are the easier it is to develop your determination and, conversely, you cannot teach an old dog new tricks!

There are no simple ways of developing determination. You can set your sights high and aim to see yourself on the winner's rostrum, but the dangers of doing this have already been touched on; lack of success may lead to demoralisation and possibly, to mediocre flying. I believe it is better to develop your determination by aiming at goals which are within your capacity – for example, the achievement of specific performances in physical exercise can prove both satisfying and confidence-boosting and this can be a good way to assert determination. It is really up to you to select an area of activity where you can practice this type of mental exercise, for that is all it is. Determination is merely an attitude of mind.

However much you want to win, and are determined to do so, you will also need to be realistic in your outlook. If you are faced with unavoidable failure then you must accept the situation. Personally, I have always found this very difficult to do and I suspect that I probably have an irrational fear of failure. However, the *realisation* of this trait in oneself is to a large extent a cure for the problem.

Perhaps the strongest sense of failure in a competitive glider pilot arises on an unscheduled out-landing. It is a very chastening experience to be firmly on the ground whilst the rest of the field are still airborne; it is also somewhat depressing, in my view, to land out on a speed task even when you know that the rest of the field have already landed and that your flight has won the day on distance alone. If, or when, you find yourself fearing the out-landing as a symbol of failure try to counter this by thinking instead of the good things about the flight; you must have enjoyed part of it at least! If this fails to raise your spirits then think instead of the good flights you have had: it is the sum of one's gliding experiences that adds up to the full enjoyment of the sport.

Physical fitness

A final area of pilot preparation to be considered is physical fitness. It is said that a healthy body begets a healthy mind and from my own experience this is completely true. I am in no doubt that if you are physically fit you are mentally far more alert than someone who fails to look after his physical condition. It is up to you how you achieve fitness, be it by jogging, press-ups, or bicycling, and to what level you aspire.

Maps

Map preparation in general was discussed in Chapter 3 but for contest work we must take the matter a stage further. I must admit that my own early competition flights not only ended with me in a sweat but were often marked by my map being left in shreds.

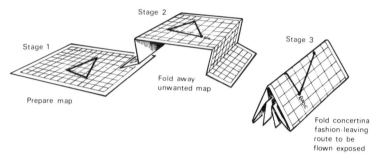

Figure 17. Map folding

The area of map I wanted to look at always seemed to be on the piece folded out of sight. A little work on this before the contest begins and before each day's flying will pay handsome dividends.

The first question to consider is how much map you need to have with you in the cockpit. On a contest flight, the answer is enough to cover the task area, but, as always, there is more to it than just that. To complete a task successfully it may be necessary to deviate off track, as we discussed in the last chapter, and so you will need to ensure that sufficient map is available in the cockpit to allow for this eventuality. I suggest you fold the map so that you have about fifteen nautical miles (thirty km) visible each side of your track line, and about ten nautical miles (twenty km) beyond the turning point.

A competition will, of course, comprise several task flights over different areas of country and so the map must encompass this entire area. Any more will be superfluous and you must consider whether to cut your map down to just the area to be flown over; cutting a map down to the minimum size to cover the task area is rather expensive but is an option you should bear in mind.

Folding a map for competitive flight needs care and forethought, but is well worth the effort. First you should fold away the parts of the map which will not be required at all during the flight, and having done this, fold the remainder so that the route to be flown is readily accessible. Figure 17 illustrates one method of doing this.

Whichever method of map folding you adopt, all the information you need for the flight should be readily available when holding the folded map in one hand. The first part of the day's task route

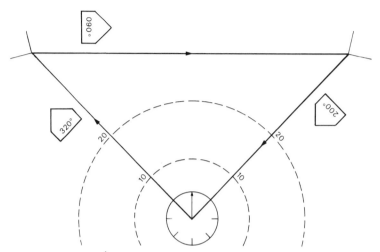

Figure 18.   Essentials of a fully prepared map

should be on the outside of the folded map and the rest should be accessible when you open one or more of the folds. Having done this, you will avoid the tendency to complete each flight with the map in a crumpled ball.

I find it useful to have a compass rose stuck over the base airfield and orientated to allow for magnetic variation, as we discussed in detail in Chapter 3. It will then be simple before the flight to read off the first magnetic track to be flown, and to determine the inbound track from the reciprocal of the bearing given by the intersection of the last leg with the rose. The intermediate track(s) can be determined by drawing a line, parallel to the tracks concerned, over the compass rose and noting the correct figure given; be careful not to take the reciprocal. As shown in Figure 18, I suggest that you write the magnetic tracks directly onto the map in pencil next to each leg of the route and close enough to each turning point for subsequent tracks to be observed before a turning point is rounded. This helps to make the turning point procedure just a little more positive and efficient.

Glider inspection

The inspection and preparation of the glider before flight is particularly important for competition work; moreover, in competition flying there can be no double standards as regards instrument and equipment serviceability. The usual checks need to be done but special attention must be paid to two aspects in particular: electrical supplies and barographs. The electricity supply is important because competition flights are long and also because of the additional demands on radio time which, of course, increases the electrical demand. In general, if there is a good twelve volts indicated from the battery under normal load then you need have no worries, but anything less is probably an indication of low battery power and a sign of potential trouble during the flight. As you will appreciate, and as I have suggested earlier, it will be worthwhile equipping the glider with a minature voltmeter as a permanent fixture in the cockpit to facilitate the monitoring of electrical supplies both before and during flight.

Many competition organisers demand a barograph trace for each day's flying as verification that the glider has not landed en route and received a fresh launch, and also to verify that the flight has not been conducted in controlled airspace. Failure to produce a trace can, in certain circumstances, result in disqualification, so barograph equipment deserves as much attention as the glider when that is the case.

The usual checks of other elements of the glider and its equipment are most important, as they are for every flight. No special consideration will be given to them here as they have been adequately covered earlier in his book.

Retrieve equipment

Competition flying involves flying many miles from base, often under difficult soaring conditions, so out-landings are a real possibility. An efficient retrieve can contribute a lot to the success of the contest. The first consideration must be to have a good crew, of one or more people, and it is more important that the individuals be reliable and conscientious than experts at gliding. Indeed, I would be so bold as to say that you should positively avoid the 'expert' as you will find that he will often claim to know, with hindsight of course, what you *should* have done on each flight. This will hardly lead to a relaxed situation and is unlikely to be conducive to successful flying.

Retrieve equipment must be in good working order so it will not be a source of worry during the competition; clearly, you need to be able to rely on your car and trailer. Don't forget that towing puts extra stress on the vehicle which can show up as cooling or transmission malfunctions. Also, remember that your car may need adjustments to its tyre inflation pressures to allow for the changed weight distribution on the car when towing. The trailer itself is, all too often, taken for granted when it really demands as much attention as the car. Tyre pressure, brakes and suspension all need checking, and when did you last check the security of the tow bar? And, of course, there are the lights. All too often trailer lights misbehave when routine servicing would eliminate the problem. The most common cause of difficulty with trailer lights is a poor earth circuit, which can frequently be caused by dampness in one of the light units. If in doubt, check the earth.

There are many aspects of checking that you can usefully do prior to competition flying but I want now to turn to the competition itself.

Know the contest area

Get to know the competition flying area before the event itself gets under way. You will find it useful to be familiar with the immediate local area especially as regards major navigational features and suitable landing areas for those final glides which do not quite work out. Naturally, it is vital to know the layout of the airfield itself because you may find yourself completing final glides at such heights that you have to land straight ahead; this is no time to wonder where it is safe to land. I find, also, that it is a useful experience to practise a few simulated final glides into the airfield in order to gain an impression of what the airfield and surrounding area looks like from a low elevation. Some places fuse into the background so well that it is easy to final glide into the wrong destination – it *has* been done, and it is very distressing to the pilot although amusing, perhaps, to his colleagues. Also, during final glides you must not rely solely upon sighting the goal but you should cross-check for precise navigation with points vertically below or immediately abeam of the glider.

Briefing

Each day's flying in a gliding competition is preceded by a briefing' at which all the pertinent information for the day's task is announced. Information given at the briefing not only satisfies one's basic needs for the task in question but can, also, prove to be part of the competition itself. I am thinking particularly of the meteorological aspects of the briefing where information is made available to all competitors but its reception and interpretation is entirely up to the individual competitor. To my mind it is essential for the serious competition pilot to attend briefing in person (some do not) and to go with the intention of extracting as much information as possible. Not only must you leave the briefing being thoroughly conversant with the task and airfield procedures but you should also have a clear idea as to how the weather is expected to behave. This latter aspect is important as tasks are generally determined from the weather anticipated and therefore any changes in the development of soaring weather during the day means that the task will prove either more, or less, demanding than the task-setters had foresawn. By watching the weather development in the period after briefing you will be able to determine how correctly it has been forecast and so you will gain an insight into how you should approach the task.

Your particular concern should be how long the task will take; knowing the anticipated thermal strength you will be able to calculate your probable average speed (see Chapter 6) and therefore your probable start and finish times. If you then observe any changes in the weather, you can check back with your original calculations.

As we discussed earlier, time spent studying the map and the route to be flown is never wasted. I like to memorise the ground features to be flown over and to make myself familiar with all aspects of the route. Not only is it sound practice to commit the magnetic headings to memory but it is useful to relate each track to a bearing relative to the sun. Remember to note possible thermal sources and think in terms of minor deviations to your route to

On the grid ready for take-off

take advantage of them. Whether you carry out this route and map study at the end of briefing or at some other time prior to launch is entirely up to you but it should, I suggest, take account of the points discussed in the next paragraph.

Final preparation

The period after briefing should be devoted to final preparation, to watching the weather develop, and to relaxation. How much time you devote to each is up to you. You yourself may find it beneficial, for example, to spend most of the time preparing the glider as a means of working off nervous energy, whereas another pilot might prefer to complete most of this preparation before briefing and to relax fully in the time available before flight. Whilst there is no general rule to suit everyone, I believe that the pilot who stands the best chance of winning will be amongst those who have made a positive effort to use the pre-flight time constructively, bearing in mind the points made throughout this chapter. Personally, I tend to use most of my time watching and assessing the weather while trying to look as if I am actually relaxing.

You will find it worthwhile getting the glider out to the launching grid well before launching commences; certainly you must avoid that last minute rush which can create distraction and so lead to accidents. I suggest, also, that you prepare the cockpit in a similar vein, placing maps in a convenient place, ensuring that the barograph is on, that you have a glide calculator, that you have taken the requisite verification photographs, etc. etc. By doing so you will be able to devote the time immediately prior to strapping in and launch to concentration on the task, to thoughts on tactics, weather and so on. Some pilots find it helpful to strap in several minutes before take-off and to use the remaining time to think about the flight. Regardless of your own approach, try to ensure that you at least have an outline plan for the flight when you take off rather than a mind bereft of any ideas at all. (It is the business of thinking positively, as we discussed before). Once you have got yourself into the frame of mind of thinking objectively about the flight it becomes easy to modify your plans in the light of circumstances. However, if you begin the flight with your mind in 'neutral' there is a good chance that it will remain in that state and you will never do better than drift around the course following other gliders. That is not the way to win.

Before taking off you will be well advised to brief your crew about where you think they should be positioned. Remember that they can play a crucial role in contributing to your success. Whether or not you use them actively during the flight, reporting on weather developments and such like, can make a difference to your final standing in the contest and you must think seriously about the pros and cons of so doing.

The main consideration is that of radio communication. To my mind you are not making proper use of your crew if you deliberately allow them to be outside radio range for a significant proportion of the flight. Clearly, there will be times when it becomes physically and technically impossible to maintain contact but as a general rule I like to be able to talk to my crew, if necessary, at any stage of the flight. They can be used to advise you on weather, and give you other information although this information will be available to other competitors unless it is reduced to a code which only you and your crew comprehend. But be careful – codes can lead to utter confusion between you and your crew if one of you does not know it adequately! Your crew also exist to give you a swift retrieve in the event of your out-landing. With good pre-landing radio procedure you can give them sufficient information to enable them to navigate directly to a point near enough to your landing spot for you to establish ground to ground radio contact. Thereafter the retrieve should be straightforward and this promptness will go some way to giving you a competitive advantage over those with more tardy crews.

Taking this a stage further, there will be times when you will need to consider sending your crew out from base to a strategic position within the task area where radio contact can be maintained. Normally you will only need to do this if the weather prospects are poor, but, beware – if your crew is too handy you may find yourself less determined to complete the course when the going becomes difficult. But, that is negative thinking; let us think of success!

Airborne

The time spent on aerotow can be used to form your initial assessment of weather conditions. The 'feel' of thermals and their frequency can be readily established on tow and it will be useful also to find out whether they seem to be well formed at low altitude. The latter may indicate how low you can afford to work the lift as a matter of routine during the flight.

Once you have released from tow I suggest you try to settle down mentally as much as possible and conserve your energies for the task itself. Spend your time sampling thermals, both near the airfield and out on the route a few miles; see how frequent they are, how easy to find and determine the height band in which you can achieve the optimum rate of climb. Clearly, you will need, also, to contact a few at relatively low altitude, say 1000 feet (300 metres), in order to obtain a complete picture.

You will then be able to modify your earlier calculation as to the length of the flight. You will be wise at this stage, however, to add an hour or so to the total to allow for the unexpected, and it is this total which you must fit into the soaring time available. If you then find that you will have soaring time to spare you must decide whether you delay your start, and by how much, so as to take advantage of the best soaring conditions. If in doubt, though, start early, because a late start leaves you no flexibility for delays or low points en route.

The flight

The start-line is invariably the scene of much gamesmanship. Whilst some pilots are quite happy to press out on the task on their own, others prefer to have a few gliders ahead of them when they themselves cross the start-line. Also, you will often find that pilots who are competing strongly will attempt to force their rivals to start first so that they can catch them up and so gain a few vital minutes on them. After that all they need to do is to pace them and finish with them and they will, perforce, have beaten them. As a budding contest pilot you may well find yourself embroiled in this little exercise, but pay no attention to it in your early contests. Certainly, don't in any way allow yourself to be upset by it but merely take note that the pundits are probably using you as a form of 'cannon-fodder'. In the fullness of time you will feel like playing the same game!

You must decide on the time to cross the start-line, bearing in mind all the factors discussed so far. You need to choose your time carefully and then make a determined effort to obtain a good start as close as possible to this time. Nothing is more frustrating than a line crossing, with all the weather cues in your favour, on which you are given a 'negative start' because you are high or wide, or otherwise in error. However, these things do happen and it will be wise to allow time in your planning for the possibility of a false start; sometimes it may only take you a few minutes to complete a second start whereas there will inevitably be times when, by reason of weather cycling, for example, it may take you thirty minutes or more to get through. In extreme cases, as when bad weather hits the airfield immediately after your abortive first crossing, you may never manage a second attempt! So, weigh up the situation carefully before you cross. At the other extreme, under very good weather it may pay you to keep making crossings until you achieve the one you consider to be near ideal. For this, do not forget that you will be looking for a crossing at maximum permitted speed and height followed by a climb to cruising height at the maximum rate, depending on the thermal conditions.

It is now time to look more closely at the tactics to use in competition. The first, and obvious, difference between flying cross-country from your home site and being in a competition is the presence of a substantial number of other gliders all flying the same route as you! This can be used to great advantage – other gliders can mark thermals and, also, when you are flying in a thermal with another glider you can assist each other by seeking out the strongest areas of lift. But, remember that gaggles of gliders frequently seem to find the weaker thermals and so if you decide to join one don't be too optimistic about thermal strength. Remember, also, that if there are several gliders in the thermal they will tend to interfere with each other's flying. You are just as likely to find a respectable core on your way to the gaggle and should be prepared to operate independently.

Don't be surprised if a glider which crossed the start-line after you catches you up and noses over to your thermal only to pass it up as being useless. The pilot may feel, quite genuinely, that he can find a better one elsewhere and it is quite likely that he is making a determined effort to overtake as many gliders as possible in the first part of the flight. You could do worse than follow the passing intruder, especially if its pilot is someone with proven ability, but be prepared for a hectic chase and for a style of flying which is probably more press-on and aggressive than yours. You will, however, find it difficult to hang on for more than part of the flight, as sooner or later you will either be left behind or you will make an alternative choice and your paths will diverge.

Whilst you should make the most of other pilots' expertise, I believe it is important to be aware that you should avoid operating for *extended* periods beyond your own capability. In other words, you should try to ignore the pundits, other than simply observing their technique, and try to fly the trip using your own judgement. Only by so doing will you learn a style that fully suits your own ability and outlook. You can, of course, learn a lot from watching other more accomplished pilots, but don't become overwhelmed. The final decision on how to fly the competition is up to you. Merely be aware of the options and the pros and cons.

Once you are out on course you have to keep reminding yourself that in a competition you can't turn back for home if the weather looks difficult, but must use all your guile to find a way round the problems. You must bear in mind that time saving is of crucial importance, but that if you are pushing on for high average speeds you run a greater risk of an out-landing than if you flew more slowly. Once again, the final decision is up to you, but I think it is probably fair to say that most people fly too cautiously and that they could afford to be more aggressive in their flying without incurring significant risk of an out-landing. This certainly applies in good weather conditions, although you must of course be more cautious when things become tricky.

If you find yourself becoming unduly bothered about a possible out-landing, try adopting a philosophical attitude and say to yourself 'what does it *really* matter if I do out-land?' The answer is, of course, that frustrating though it may be to suffer an out-landing, it does not matter at all. You will have ruined your chances in that particular competition but next time your ill-luck may strike someone else instead. So, my advice is to go right ahead and not worry about an out-landing – just get on with the flying in a determined style.

Many pilots find their composure seriously upset when they get low during a contest flight. This is also often associated with concern about out-landing but, once again, clear thinking can be of assistance. Consider a winch or car launch, when the height achieved is often in the order of 1000 feet (300 metres) only : in such circumstances a competent pilot flying a high performance glider would, on a soarable day, be unlucky not to contact lift and climb away. Indeed, the initial thermal is often not found until well below launch height. So, when on a competition flight you find yourself getting low just remember all the times you have thought nothing special about climbing away after a winch launch. I find it a consoling thought! It may also help you if you consider a further reason for this concern, which is that in a contest the usual launch height is 2000 feet (600 metres) and as most of the flight is conducted above this it tends to become regarded as the minimum height. In reality 2000 feet is well above a reasonable minimum and should only be regarded as a height at which you might be prepared to accept weaker thermals. Obviously, there will be exceptions : there will be days when thermals are strong at low heights, when it will pay to work down low but equally there will be days, especially when the wind is strong, when getting below even 3000 feet will spell difficulty.

When an out-landing becomes inevitable you should try to remember all the points learnt in your earlier flying, particularly with regard to leaving yourself adequate height to select a suitable field and to carry out a considered approach and landing. It is all too easy to get carried away and keep flying when the chips are clearly down and things are beyond you; you must resist the temptation to press on and you should, instead, concentrate on the landing. If you break your glider in a competition out-landing you will have to drop out of the rest of the event : it is much better to keep the machine and yourself intact and live to fight another day.

On some contest flights nothing seems to go right; gliders overtake you, you drop out of thermals and your morale suffers. Rest assured, this is a common occurrence and it happens to everyone at some time. There are three, likely reactions; you ignore the situation and carry on as though nothing were amiss, you feel pessimistic and are inclined to give up the struggle, or you panic, wanting to throw reason to the wind and press on and stay with the gliders ahead at all costs.

There is not much to say about the first two reactions, although defeatism is not an attitude of mind you should allow to persist. But panic needs discussion. The desire to hang on to the gliders ahead of you can become so strong that your tactical judgement becomes clouded; for instance in a thermal with gliders well above you, you may leave when they do, instead of taking the climb to the optimum height. By doing so you may remain in the same geographic position as them but your lower height can mean that you are in a different ball-game tactically. If you persist you run the risk of dropping below the height band of optimum lift altogether and this will put you even further behind the other gliders. In extreme cases it will put you on the ground. Clearly, you should fly your own tactics, and with a modicum of good fortune you may find a thermal strong enough to enable you to catch the other gliders in due course. But this takes discipline. There are no hard and fast rules about what height difference constitutes a tactical separation from other gliders, but think in terms of 1000 feet (300 metres) rather than in hundreds of feet. The precise difference will, amongst other things, depend upon depth of convection and thermal distribution.

When national regulations permit it, you may consider cloud flying in competitions. The subject is an emotive one which often brings a storm of comment from people in countries which do not permit cloud flying by gliders. Those of us who fly in Great Britain are fortunate in being allowed freedom to cloud fly when out of controlled airspace and this is so in contest flying, too. When cloud flying, the regulations for height separation through radio contact are particularly important if collision risks are to be reduced. However, the need for cloud flying in competitions is, to my mind, minimal and, whilst it is pleasant to have the freedom to do so, I believe it is seldom of any real tactical advantage with a modern glass-fibre machine. Psychologically it is a grand feeling to make a cloud climb and to have all that height under you but the disappointment comes when you set out on your straight glide from the cloud. Water droplets or, worse still, ice on the wing ruin your glider's performance and bring it down to a glide angle more appropriate to a basic training machine than to a high performance

Opposite – dawn of a good soaring day

contest type. Whilst your rate of climb may be agreeably fast in a cloud climb you may well lose, by a degraded glide, the time saved in the climb. (On the other hand, if you have to cross a wide gap of non-soarable air then a cloud climb may well be the only way to get across.) On balance, though, I believe you are normally better off staying below cloud where you can fully exploit the glider's performance and also take account of the changing tactical situation. Moreover, remember that clouds are more easily assessed from below than from above and this, to my mind, militates against cloud flying.

If you do find it expedient to cloud fly in a contest then you will need to pay special attention to navigation. First, the winds at height may be much stronger than at the operating levels below cloud and your drift with the wind may catch you unawares. If your flight is into wind you may well find that additional drift from the stronger winds up aloft prevents any gain from a cloud climb. The answer is to know the wind speed and direction at typical cloud flying heights on the day in question and to take note of the time you spend in cloud; this will at least give you a reasonable chance of keeping a continuous check on your position. The second point to bear in mind is that you must maintain the desired heading accurately when leaving cloud. If you fail to straighten up on or near the intended heading when leaving the lift in cloud then you will, again, lose some of the advantage you may have gained by going up into cloud, and if you allow yourself to wander off heading whilst flying blind you will have additional losses. Altogether you should think twice, at least, before you elect to climb in cloud during a contest.

We have discussed the various facets of rounding a turning point in some detail in earlier chapters but there is one new aspect which needs covering at this stage – collision risk. In a competition, with so many gliders flying the same course, it is common for several to be in the vicinity of a turning point at the same time which clearly means that the risk of collision is greater than normal. Therefore, pay particular attention to looking out for other gliders as you approach and round each turning point.

Finally, let's think about the end of the flight. There are two common problems with final glides in contests; the first arises from an unnecessarily conservative approach to flying which leads to excessive height over the finish line or to excessive speed through trying to lose this height. Clearly, this is inefficient in competitive terms. The second and tactically more significant problem arises from the sheer excitement of the situation; you may find yourself tempted to glide for the finish line with barely sufficient height to reach it in a straight glide. This is a perfectly reasonable thing to do if there is plenty of lift en route but is risky if the thermal conditions are uncertain. My advice here is to try and keep a cool head and continue to think rationally. Finally, remember that a landing short of the finish line is of little value as far as your score is concerned; I believe it is normally best to err on the cautious side and always have a little height to spare, whenever possible.

Finally, a word about scores. You will find, all too often, that you have flown what you believe to be an excellent flight and yet when the scores are published you find yourself well down the placings. This is a common occurrence and happens to the very best, so be consoled. However, what it can illustrate is how important saving time is in competitive racing gliding. The pilot who wins most consistently is the one who habitually saves the greatest accumulation of seconds; this comes from persistent application of the principles of efficient flying augmented by that one combination for which there is no substitute – experience boosted by a little bit of luck.

In this chapter I have probably not answered all the questions which you may have. I hope I may have given you an appreciation of some of the more common and more important factors which contribute to success in a competition. The rest is up to you!

8
Getting the most out of your glider

Soaring in a glider which has not been properly prepared will put you at an obvious disadvantage. Most glider pilots keep their machines clean and polished but I am surprised by the lack of understanding often displayed of the more fundamental aspects of glider preparation which have a real and significant bearing on performance.

The modern glass-fibre glider is manufactured with high standards of accuracy. In particular, the wing profile is made to an accuracy which is not easily achieved with other structural materials.

A glider wing, or indeed any part of the machine, will work best when its local air flow is not spoilt by turbulence arising from air leaking through or between parts of the structure. Flight tests have consistently shown that an accurate wing profile has a significant bearing on the performance which the glider can achieve and it has been demonstrated that irregularities of or on the surface of the profile can bring about a marked reduction in achieved performance. By attention to both these points – air leakage and wing profile – measurable gains in performance can be realised.

In this chapter we will look first at leakage which is perhaps the easier problem to solve. We will then look very briefly at the task of ensuring that the wing profile is smooth, which is rather more complex.

Before turning to the practical remedies of air leakage around a glider structure, it will be helpful to remind ourselves of the typical distribution of pressure around a machine in flight.

Pressure distribution

For all practical purposes, air flowing at low speeds can be considered as incompressible, with a relationship of pressure multiplied

Most glider pilots keep their machines clean and polished!

by velocity being proportional to a constant holding true. Referring to Figure 19, consider a parcel of air as it encounters a streamlined body. The greater curvature of the upper surface means that the portion of air which travels around it has further to go to meet up with the portion which has passed along the lower surface. Because the air travelling around the upper surface has further to go it must accelerate to meet up at the trailing edge with the air which has passed underneath. Referring to the relationship between pressure and velocity mentioned above, we can see that this increase in velocity must be associated with a reduction in pressure.

Whenever air flows past *any* streamline body it experiences a local acceleration which results in a pressure drop in relation to ambient conditions. As the air completes its passage over the body it decelerates and the pressure returns to ambient. This general rule holds good when considering airflow around a glider, although there are other facets of low-speed airflow which I am neglecting because they are not relevant here.

With a glider wing, these pressure changes give us a pressure below ambient above the upper surface of the aerofoil with a

117

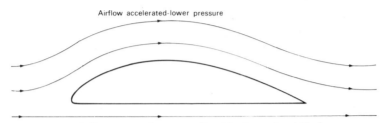

Airflow accelerated-lower pressure

Figure 19.   Airflow around a streamlined body – simplified

pressure near ambient below. This variation in pressure between the two surfaces of an aerofoil provides the basis of aerodynamic lift, but it also encourages air to leak through or between elements of the structure and so to degrade performance. The pressure differential which we have described will induce air to flow from the lower surface to the upper surface of a glider wing, and the unsealed junction between a wing and a fuselage, or the hinge line of ailerons and flaps would be just the route it would try to pass through.

Pressure changes also take place around a fuselage. Because of the shape of the cockpit, air flowing over this area will accelerate, which again will result in a local reduction in pressure. Here, drag can easily be created by allowing air of relatively high pressure in the cockpit to leak out into the low pressure air outside through gaps around the canopy, the wing roots, and the undercarriage. This situation is very common because the air taken into the cockpit from the nose of the glider for ventilation purposes is already at a relatively high pressure. Naturally, any leakage around the smooth profile of the fuselage, especially the forward portion, will disturb the surrounding airflow and produce drag.

There are other implications arising from ventilation which will be discussed later in this chapter.

The degree of pressure change around a wing profile which is generating lift is substantially greater than that around a fuselage, because a fuselage is not designed to produce lift. This means that air leakage is more likely with a wing and as the wing is responsible for such a large proportion of a glider's total drag, any small increase in drag from the wing from leakage, and the disturbance of the laminar flow pattern which it causes, will have a significant effect on performance.

For practical work on glider sealing you can determine general pressure distribution from a straightforward assessment of the glider's form. More about pressure distribution will be found on p. 127.

Sealing

First, we will look at sealing the wing. The first aim must be to block the obvious routes air will take from the lower surface to the upper, as it tries to gain equilibrium. These routes are the aileron, and the flap hinge lines, and also the airbrakes, if they are of the 'paddle' type.

There are three types of aileron/flap commonly used on gliders: the surface hinged, the centre hinged and the inset hinge (Frieze). Each type requires separate treatment for sealing. Additionally, there is the Fowler flap, as used on the Blanik, but this should definitely not be sealed as it operates by way of the slot created between the flap leading edge and the rear of the mainplane itself when the flaps are extended.

Flaps/ailerons

The *surface hinged* mechanism is easy to seal and you need only a length of fabric backed tape to do this. There are many examples of gliders so equipped ranging from the little Ka 6 through to the Nimbus 2 and ASW 17. Figure 20 illustrates a typical installation.

On delivery these gliders will all be correctly taped, but you must keep a check on this; even taped surfaces can produce drag if the tape covering the gap is sucked into the airflow by the pressure distribution around that area.

It is surprising how often one sees elderly aircraft flown without any control sealing tape having been fitted. The airflow will therefore be disturbed over the control surface and in extreme circumstances, this may reduce the effectiveness of the controls.

Control surface tape should be replaced before it starts to peel off with age. Before attempting to remove old tape it is a good idea to soften the adhesive by coating the outer surface of the tape with a

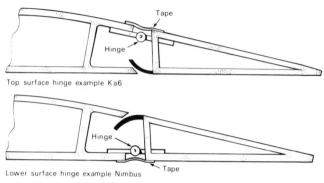

Figure 20.   Surface hinged control surface

suitable solvent and allowing it to permeate through to the adhesive itself. On glass-fibre gliders finished in a gelcoat almost any common solvent can be used without risk of damage to the glider surface; the most effective is acetone, but a more readily available liquid is cellulose thinner. On gliders finished in conventional paints or cellulose dopes great care must be taken to find a solvent which will not damage the glider's paintwork. If in doubt ask someone who knows, before you ruin your glider's finish in a fit of zealous enthusiasm.

The tape should be pulled off slowly, with the hand held as close as possible to the surface of the structure. If it is pulled off hastily or at, say, 90° to the surface, chunks of glider finish will probably come off with the tape. Very depressing.

You will then need to clean the area on which the fresh tape is to be applied, using the same solvent as before. Once this has been done you are ready to set about sticking the fresh tape on to the glider, but first lay the wing horizontal, as this greatly simplifies the task. The next step is to fully deflect the control surfaces away from the surface to be taped; failure to do this will result in restricted control movement, once retaped. The new tape should then be applied carefully, ensuring that it lies in a straight line and is symmetrical about the hinge axis. The control surface should then be returned to the zero deflection position and the slack tape along the hinge line should be pushed into the gap between the wing and the control surface. This will ensure that the slack tape, present

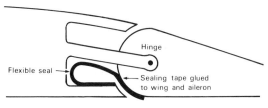

Figure 21.   Centre/inset hinge control

when other than full control deflection is applied, is folded away out of the airflow. The final step is to check that the controls have freedom of movement, and it is worth repeating this check after the glider has been rigged.

A less common type of control surface is the *centre hinged* but this has been overtaken in a number of gliders by a similar but more effective design, the *inset hinged* which is also known as a Frieze control surface. We will consider how to seal the inset hinged type, though this method may also be used with the centre hinged, such as those fitted in Libelle and Kestrel gliders. Figure 21 illustrates the essentials.

Some of the latest gliders, such as the Ventus and Nimbus 3, have a control system which uses a similar method of sealing.

Although seals should have a relatively long life, it will be necessary from time to time to remove flaps and ailerons which will mean you have to re-fit the seals. The best procedure I have found for fitting such seals is as follows. Support the wing vertically, with its leading edge towards the ground, and deflect the flaps and ailerons fully down. Draw a pencil line along the bottom surface of these controls, using the trailing edge of the wing skin to guide the pencil, as shown in Figure 22.

The controls should then be removed and their leading edges cleaned with degreaser and abraded back to the pencil line. (This line represents the limit of the gluing surface for the tape.) It will be worthwhile applying masking tape along the surface to the rear of the pencil line so as to protect the surface which you do not wish to be abraded. The lower surface of the wing skin, inside the U channel at the rear of the wing, should be cleaned and abraded also, see Figure 23.

There are various fabrics suitable for seals. Generally speaking, a

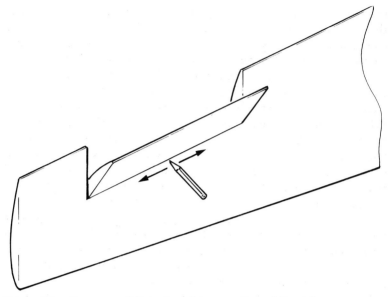

Figure 22.   Draw pencil line along lower surface of flap/ailerons

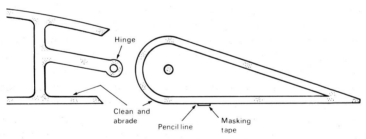

Figure 23.   Cleaning and abrasion of gluing surfaces

thick close-woven fabric type which is non-porous to air will be satisfactory. The tape should be cut into strips about 80mm wide (if not supplied in approximately that width) and into lengths which are easily managed – say about 1.5 metres. However, it is preferable to cut the length to that of the control surface being sealed if you can manage this. The surfaces of the tape which are to be glued should be very lightly abraded to provide a key for the adhesive. A thin layer of strong contact (impact) adhesive can be applied to the abraded surface in the U channel of the wing trailing edge and on the corresponding surface of the tape. The tape can then be glued to the inside of the U channel, so that the unsecured edge faces the leading edge of the wing. When fastened, this unsecured edge should be pulled out of the channel and then bent over the rear edge of the wing and taped back over the lower surface so that it is kept out of the way whilst the control surfaces are re-attached. The control surfaces can now be refitted. With the surfaces deflected fully up their abraded lower surfaces should be lightly coated with adhesive, as should the exposed surface of the sealing tape. (As an alternative to adhesive you can use double-sided sticky tape, which saves time.) The sealing tape can then be pulled tight and attached to the control surface, but take care not to cause creases or air bubbles in or under the tape. The control should now be fully deflected down and, using the wing trailing edge as a guide, a knife should be worked very lightly down the wing to cut off surplus tape – the line of the cut will coincide with the earlier pencil line. The surfaces should be checked for freedom of movement before the glider is rigged for flight.

Two details should be considered when fitting these seals. First, the seals will act as water traps which, in icing conditions, could restrict control movement. Drain holes in the seal should therefore be provided at each hinge; note that the glider's dihedral will cause water to run inboard to each hinge position. Second, the flap seals, once fitted, can continue to remain attached to the wing section itself because, to remove the controls, it will only be necessary to unstick the tape in contact with the controls themselves. It might, therefore, be prudent to use a long life or ultra-strong impact adhesive to attach the seal to the wing itself, whereas an ordinary household impact adhesive can be used on the controls. Bear in mind, however, the merits of using double sided PVC sticky tape or similar materials instead of conventional adhesive.

Airbrakes

Airbrakes can be sources of appreciable air leakage and consequent loss of performance. Many of the latest racing gliders are fitted with trailing edge flap/airbrakes and these can readily be sealed with tape, as described above, although the gap between the airbrake and the flap can also be sealed to minimise performance losses. However, the older gliders having paddle type brakes require specific treatment, and may be considered in two broad categories, those with brakes on both the top and bottom surfaces and those with top surface brakes only. The more recent types of glider with paddle type airbrakes are, however, normally fitted with airbrakes which are mounted in the wings in sealed boxes, so they don't need to be sealed.

An installation with both top and bottom paddles is hard to seal, though. Moreover, if both top and bottom paddles on each wing are fitted into the same box structure as each other, so that there is an unobstructed air passage through the box when both brakes are open, then it is very difficult to seal them effectively. Most sealing installations I have seen have been incorporated on the top surface paddle only which exacerbates the problem. Unfortunately, in flight the wing distorts and the lift on the top surface paddle will counter the effect of the airtight seal by easing the close fit achieved when on the ground. Therefore, it is probably best to seal the lower paddle as then the natural pressure distribution in flight will ensure that the lower one stays firmly against its seal.

But caution – sealing airbrakes can lead to restricted operation, and you need to be especially careful when you do this.

If it is the lower surface paddle which is to be sealed, it is best to de-rig the glider and lay the wing horizontally with its lower surface uppermost. The airbrakes should then be opened and the surfaces of the paddle which are in contact with the wing when closed given one coat of release agent or non-silicone wax. The surfaces of the airbrake box the paddle rests against when the airbrakes are closed should be lightly abraded and de-greased ready for the application of a sealing compound. The edges of the airbrake paddle cap are then covered with one thickness of Dymo tape, or similar, so that the tape does not protrude below the lower edge of the cap. This tape ensures that a gap remains between the paddle cap and the airbrake box even if surplus sealing compound squeezes into the region. When all this has been done, a layer of two-part rubberised sealant or, less satisfactorily, silicone rubber (bathtub sealant), should be applied to those surfaces of the airbrake box the paddle rests against when closed. The airbrakes are then locked shut in this position either by simulating the closing force on the actuating mechanism at the wing root, or by rigging the glider and locking the airbrakes shut. See Figure 24.

The airbrakes should not be unlocked until the sealant has fully

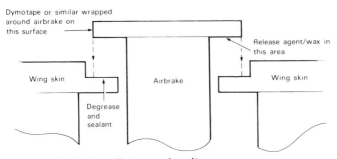

Figure 24. Airbrake installation and sealing

set, because to do so earlier will distort the seal before it has fully hardened; forty-eight hours should be sufficient for the material to solidify, in normal temperate conditions. Once set, the airbrakes should be unlocked and gently levered open at the paddle itself. On no account should they be forced open by the airbrake actuating mechanism as this will over-load the system and perhaps cause damage. A 50 mm wide metal spatula or strip of thin dural can be used, eased gently under the paddle cap at one end in order to break the release agent. Once one end has been lifted, the rest of the paddle will free readily, and the Dymo tape can then be removed.

The glider should now be rigged and checked for satisfactory operation of the airbrakes. To be certain that the brakes will function properly the wing should be flexed to simulate the inflight bending. Naturally, the flight test should be conducted carefully in case over-zealous sealing results in an airbrake mal-function.

Sealing airbrakes fitted on the upper surfaces alone can be done in the same way. However, it will probably be simpler to tackle the problem by preventing air passing into the wing in the first place; check the wing root rib and the holes in the rear of the wing which carry the actuating rods to determine the likely course for leaking air. Remember that such flow should only occur when the holes are in a relatively high pressure area.

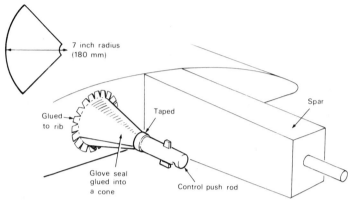

Figure 25.   Glove seal

Glove seals

The procedure for sealing the wing root is straightforward and can be used in several other parts of the glider. Normally, the only air passages in the wing root are those around the various control rods and the sealing process involves making glove-type seals which fit around the rod and are glued to the face of the rib.

The glove seals should be cut from a piece of fine grade sail-cloth or chamois leather. Particular patterns will naturally vary from installation to installation, but Figure 25 illustrates a basic pattern. When cut, the glove should be made into a cone, and glued along the edge with impact/contact adhesive. The apex of the cone should be trimmed to achieve a tight fit over the push rod in question, and the base should be cut along the axis of the cone to provide 15 mm long flaps which can be folded outwards and glued to the face of the wing root rib. The apex of the glove should then be wrapped with PVC tape so that it fits tightly on the push rod.

Fuselage ventilation

Air taken into the cockpit for ventilation creates drag. Consider a small parcel of air, passing the glider in flight, and allowed to enter the cockpit. The movement is immediately retarded, and reduction in speed of the air parcel brings about drag overall to the glider. There is nothing we can do to alter this fact, but we can alleviate its effects. The most obvious way is to use ventilation sparingly, but, other than appreciating that drag can be saved thereby, it is really a non-solution. There are, however, two practical ways of reducing ventilation related drag slightly; one is to provide an easy path through the fuselage for ventilation air, so reducing the degree to which it is retarded, and the other is to prevent air taken into the cockpit from leaking out of the fuselage at various junctions and disturbing local airflow.

Air will naturally flow from a high to a low pressure area, and you can take advantage of this fact by providing an exit for ventilation air in the fuselage at a point where there is relatively low pressure. Some manufacturers provide these exits at the tail in the form of reversed air scoops or with a suitable gap in the base of the fin/rudder junction, and it may be possible to modify your glider with similar devices. However, in almost every case this will involve cutting holes in structural parts and you must contact an expert, preferably the manufacturer or his repair agent, before attempting such work. An alternative location for an exit is on the side of the fuselage, again using a reversed air scoop. The location of such an exit must be determined by local air pressures; you also need to consider the drag created by the device itself, which will protrude on the glider. Again, you must seek expert opinion as to where a suitable hole may be safely made in the fuselage.

Pressure measurement

Local air pressures on the fuselage surface can be determined experimentally by taping a number of polythene pipes to the skin of the fuselage where you think it suitable to place an air extraction orifice, and routing the other ends of the pipes to the cockpit through the canopy DV panel. The pipes on the outside of the aircraft should be laid approximately parallel to the fuselage datum, and a small hole (1 mm) should be made in the outer facing surface of each pipe, and the ends should be sealed. Each pipe should be lettered or numbered for identification. A flight test can then be conducted, during which a highly sensitive pressure gauge capable of reading at reduced pressures, is carried in the cockpit and connected in turn to each pipe. A record of the readings obtained will show the area of the lowest relative pressure and so the best point for any proposed exit. Naturally, the measurements should all be made at the same airspeed.

This method of measuring pressures can be adapted for use on other parts of the glider.

Fuselage sealing

The final task on the fuselage is to determine the places where ventilation air may escape and to seal them fully. The wing root is one area notorious for drag caused by air leakage and therefore the wing fuselage junction should always be taped. If the canopy fits over the wing, as on the Libelle or Kestrel, its junction with the wing should be sealed with non-porous foam rubber. Another area of leakage is around the canopy and fuselage junction and this too can be sealed with a very thin strip of foam rubber. Alternatively, it can be sealed in a similar way to that described for airbrake paddles, with the proviso that this solution is only suitable for use in temperatures similar to those pertaining when the silicone rubber seal was applied. The reason is that the canopy perspex and aircraft structure expand and contract at differing rates with temperature changes, and, under adverse conditions, the canopy will develop either too tight or too loose a fit. A better solution is to fit the canopy rail with a soft PVC or rubber tube which will act as an adjustable seal. This tube can also be inflated once the canopy is closed to provide an even better seal. However, as with drilling holes for air extraction, expert advice should be sought before a channel is cut in the canopy rail for such a tube. The cockpit rim itself is a signficant structural part and the canopy frame may also not take kindly to having some of its material removed.

Finally, areas such as undercarriage doors and junctions of fins and tailplanes can be sealed with worthwhile results. The method used will depend upon the nature of each particular job, but you will generally find those described above to be suitable. If you seal your fuselage particularly well you will probably find that you will then *have* to ensure there is adequate air extraction, using one of the methods already discussed. In most gliders a well sealed fuselage will virtually stop the usual ad-hoc 'natural leakage' ventilation system working, as the air quite simply will have nowhere to go. This indicates that, before sealing, air was probably leaking out of all sorts of undesirable places and this may well be the first tangible indication that your efforts at sealing have worked. You will be surprised how quiet a well sealed glider can become; a quiet glider is one which is operating efficiently, and that is really the name of the game.

Smoothing the wing

If you really want to go to town on improving your glider you can usefully have a go at smoothing the wing surfaces. With increasing age all gliders develop blemishes on their wings which can spoil laminar airflow, and so increase drag and reduce performance. Glass or carbon fibre gliders are no exception as, with age, the resins used continue to shrink and cause small distortions in the skin.

We will only consider the elimination of small defects on glass or carbon fibre gliders, as the problems of more extensive profiling work are too great to tackle here.

The first thing you need to acquire is a quantity of 600 grade 'wet and dry' abrasive paper with a smaller quantity of 800 grade and also 1200 grade. Some cutting paste, as used to bring up the paint-work on motor vehicles, will also be useful. Next, you will need a rubbing block with which to hold the 'wet and dry' in even contact with the wing. A 12 inch long piece of $1'' \times 2''$ timber, absolutely straight, with a piece of $\frac{1}{4}''$ thick hard rubber glued to the $2''$ wide surface as backing for the 'wet and dry' is a practical and easily made rubbing block. There are more sophisticated devices available, but this will suffice for our purposes.

Before setting to work on the wing you must appreciate that the gel coat on a glider is only about $\frac{1}{2}$ mm thick and, therefore, over-zealous work with the 'wet and dry' will produce grey patches where the colour of the cloth shows through the much-thinned gel coat. If you rub down to this extent you are in a whole new ball game, and you will have to paint fresh gel coat onto the wing and then wet and dry that down.

Starting with the 600 grade, then – either wrap a sheet of 'wet and dry' around the rubbing block or, with double sided adhesive tape, glue a strip of it on to the rubber faced surface. With a sponge, wet the immediate wing surface to be cut back, and then work the rubbing block chordwise in long steady strokes, interspersed with some at $45°$ to the chord. Always ensure that the block lies flat on

End of a soaring day

the wing and that pressure is evenly applied, and also keep wetting the wing surface to ensure that gel coat removed by the abrasive is washed off. You will be able to feel the improvements to the wing surface by lightly running your hand over the area which has been worked on; alternatively, a thin coat of grey cellulose paint sprayed on to the wing before work commences will be a good guide as to when high spots have been removed.

Wear waterproof gloves whilst handling the 'wet and dry' if you value the skin on your finger tips.

When the 600 grade has produced a smooth surface you merely polish up with 800 grade, followed by 1200. The final gloss is applied by cutting paste and much elbow grease – it really is almost that simple. I say 'almost' because there are little tricks which can be used to simplify the process but you will learn these quite readily as you progress.

It is all well worth the effort; a good wing and a good sealing job and you will detect a small but persistent improvement in performance. And, what is more, it is very satisfying. It will also give you a good head-start in your progress towards successful competitive gliding; you will know that your machine is on top line and this can be of major psychological benefit.

In my own case I have always gone to great lengths to ensure that the glider I plan to fly in a competition is in tip-top condition; the very act of working on the machine and improving it in as many ways as possible does much to give me confidence. I know that I am getting the most out of it and that the rest of the competitive exercise is entirely up to me. In other words, I always aim to have complete confidence in my glider – it does much to improve my own performance. I am sure it will work for you.

Successful competition gliding demands the utmost discipline in a pilot; self-discipline, discipline in the preparation of the glider and all equipment, discipline when making decisions in the air especially when balancing the desire to win with flight safety. No matter what the stakes, an injured pilot and a broken glider is too high a price to pay for what should be fun. Competition gliding *is* great fun, but it is a sport which is unforgiving to the rash and careless, and which demands nothing less than the very best from all participants.

Index

Index